250 YEARS OF BREWING IN IPSWICH

Overleaf: Thomas Cobbold (1680-1752) set up the brewery at Harwich in 1723 and moved his brewing operations to Ipswich in 1746. This painting hangs in the offices of Heyman Barwell Jones in Ipswich.

250 YEARS OF BREWING IN IPSWICH

The story of Tollemache and Cobbold's Cliff Brewery, 1746 - 1996

By

Robert Malster

MALTHOUSE PRESS IN ASSOCIATION WITH
TOLLEMACHE & COBBOLD BREWERY LTD. 1996

Published by
Malthouse Press in association with
Tollemache & Cobbold Brewery Ltd.
ISBN 0 9522355 3 6

British Library Cataloguing - in - Publication Data
A catalogue record for this book is available from the British Library

Designed by Robert Malster
Printed in Great Britain by
The Wolsey Press,
Ipswich, Suffolk IP3 9QR

Contents

Front cover: Cliff Brewery in a painting by Terry Jeffrey, 1991.

Back cover: A painting by Fred Russell of the old brewery, much of which dated from 1746.

Foreword

by Sir John Harvey-Jones

A RECENT study of businesses showed that the average life of a firm would now be only forty years. A firm that has carried on in the same place in the same broad line of business for a hundred years is totally exceptional.

It says something for the enduring characteristics of the product and the dogged determination of the local customers not to be cheated and not to have their favourite brew moved, that the Tolly Cobbold brewery is still surviving after two hundred and fifty years in the business.

Needless to say no business survives that length of time without constant change, including changes of ownership. It looked as though the end of the line had been reached in July, 1989. The brewery was closed for what proved, in the event, to be a one-year interregnum, but thanks to Brian Cowie and Bob Wales, who courageously led a management buyout, the old vats were in business again by July, 1990.

I first met Brian and Bob when it was suggested that their story might prove an interesting feature film for the BBC *Troubleshooter* series. Moreover, the two of them were flat out for any ideas or suggestions which would improve their chances of survival.

Brian and Bob combine hard-headed realistic business skills with a vision, imagination and commitment to Ipswich and the surrounding area that is heartening to see. The dedication that the two of them have given to the area has been matched by the support from Ipswich Borough Council and the people of Suffolk. The Tolly Cobbold brewery now forms a part of the Ipswich Heritage Trail, and the refurbished Brewery Tap pub has had to be expanded to cope with the demand.

At a time when breweries everywhere are having a tough time, Brian and Bob have continued to invest for the future in which they have high hopes. It is this combination of a dream of the future with the hard-nosed skills of running a business which Thomas Cobbold showed in 1746 when he transferred his brewing enterprise from Harwich to Ipswich. He would, I believe, be proud to see what has been achieved, and would join me in wishing Brian and Bob and the brewery continued success.

The pump clip for Tolly Bitter contains an artist's view of Cliff Brewery and the Brewery Tap, formerly Cliff House – a Cobbold residence.

Acknowledgements

Robert Malster

THE WRITING of a book is by no means a solitary occupation. However many lonely hours an author spends at the typewriter or the word processor keyboard, he also spends many hours talking to those who provide him with information, illustrations, advice and other help.

This short history of an important Suffolk business, now celebrating the 250th anniversary of brewing in Ipswich, would never have been completed without the involvement of a good many people, and it is a great pleasure as well as a duty to acknowledge their input to the book. First of all my thanks go to Brian Cowie and Bob Wales, the joint managing directors of Tollemache & Cobbold Brewery Ltd., for inviting me to write this history, and for their confidence in me at times when progress was painfully slow. I must thank them, too, for their patience as they explained to me the background to the reopening of the brewery. I am grateful also to the Hon. Peter Strutt, chairman of Tollemache & Cobbold Brewery Ltd., for his help.

Stan Clarke gave me a valuable flavour of life in the Tollemache and Cobbold breweries over the years, and head brewer Chris Gregson was generous with his time initiating me into the intricacies of the brewing process. An old friend, Stuart Bowell, of CAMRA, helped me to avoid any number of errors in the writing.

A number of people helped with the supply of illustrations, among them John Wilton and Mrs S. Pegg. Mr P. M. Hope Cobbold most kindly made it possible for us to photograph a number of the family portraits and other paintings at Glemham Hall, and Mr Richard Cobbold made available the portrait of Thomas Cobbold which forms the frontispiece. For his work in copying many of these pictures I am indebted to my old friend and colleague, John Loughton. I am most grateful to the Editor of the East Anglian Daily Times, Malcolm Pheby, for permission to use a number of photographs taken for that newspaper.

Finally, I must express my gratitude to Sir John Harvey -Jones for so willingly consenting to write a foreword and to the Hon. Peter Strutt for providing a postscript.

Introduction

IT WAS a sombre gathering that evening in July, 1989, at the Cliff Brewery. Pub landlords and landladies who had known the brewery and sold its beer for many a year had gathered to mourn the loss of a very significant part of local life in Suffolk.

Leisure group Brent Walker had decided for economic reasons to close the Ipswich brewery and transfer all production to their other brewery, the Lion Brewery at Hartlepool. It was the end of brewing at the Cliff after 243 years, and the end of brewing in Ipswich after uncounted centuries.

The Victorian brewery was to be demolished to make way for redevelopment, and the equipment was to be scrapped, apart from some historic items which were, it was rumoured, to be taken to Hartlepool to form part of a brewing museum there. More than sixty people, some of whom had served the brewery all their working lives, were to lose their jobs.

It was, everybody agreed sadly, the end of an era. Many a salty tear was shed into the beer that night.

Yet it was not the end for the Cliff Brewery or for Tolly Cobbold. It was truly the end of one era, but another was soon to begin in which the brewery, for so long a landmark on the Orwell shore, was to play an extended role as a working museum as well as being a working brewery.

Today, 250 years after the brewing business of Thomas Cobbold was transferred to the Cliff from Harwich, visitors come from far and wide to see how beer is produced in a building which is very much a part of Suffolk history, and to sample drinks produced to traditional recipes.

This book is not just the story of the brewing enterprise of two Suffolk families, the Cobbolds and the Tollemaches, but tells also of how a Suffolk business arose like a phoenix from the ashes of its former existence. It is not just a tale of past business activity but also an inspiring one of men who in the 1990s were prepared to swim against the tide of recession to achieve their vision of a new life for a wonderful brewery, its tradition and heritage, which has played so important a part in the lives of the people of Suffolk and beyond.

The move to Ipswich 1

THE YEAR was 1746. On 16th April the Duke of Cumberland, third son of King George II, had routed the Young Pretender's highlanders at Culloden, on Drummossie Muir in Inverness-shire, bringing an end to the rebellion of '45 and the hopes of the house of Stuart to regain the throne.

Abroad, Peru's chief port, Callao, was destroyed by an earthquake and accompanying tidal wave, and 6,000 people died. A little nearer home, the Austrians occupied the ancient port city of Genoa, but were driven out by a rising led by a boy named Ballila.

And much nearer home, Thomas Cobbold transferred his brewing enterprise from the Essex port of Harwich to a site beside the Orwell in Ipswich, thus solving at a stroke one of the problems that had beset him ever since he had set up a brewery in King's Quay Street, Harwich, twenty-three years earlier.

Thomas was a maltster, skilled in turning the barley grown on East Anglian farms into good malt for the brewer's mash tun. He had been born in 1680, a descendant of one Robert Cobbold, of Tostock, yeoman, whose death is recorded in 1603. Robert's grandson Reynold died at Rattlesden in 1666, the year of the Great Fire of London, at the age of 102, and it was Reynold's grandson John who was Thomas's father.

When in 1723 Thomas Cobbold turned to brewing and started up his Harwich brewery he quickly found that the local water was distinctly brackish, because salt water tended to seep into the town's wells owing to the fact that the town was almost entirely surrounded by the sea. The quality of the water, or liquor as the brewer tends to call it, is vital to the brewer; he cannot make good beer with unsatisfactory water.

Thomas had the answer to that problem; he imported his liquor from the crystal-clear springs of Holywells, an estate close to the River Orwell just below Ipswich which was in the hands of the Cobbold family.

Thomas Gainsborough painted a view of the town from Holywells during his years in Ipswich, showing the three lakes into which the water ran on its way down towards the Orwell. This suggests that the artist was on good terms with the Cobbolds, who might well have given him special permission to work on their estate.

To bring the water to Harwich he had employed a fleet of water schuyts, or shoots as the English sailors called them; wooden sailing vessels with tanks and large manual pumps for emptying them. It is said that the same vessels brought beer brewed at the Harwich brewery back to Ipswich, but one cannot imagine the tanks were simply filled with beer; a good brewer took much better care of his

Opposite page: Holywells, home of the Cobbold family for many years and the source of the water on which their trade was founded; a photograph from a family album.

beer than that, and it is more likely that casks of beer were stacked on deck for the return journey.

The transportation of sweet water from the Holywells enabled Thomas Cobbold to make excellent beer at Harwich, but the transport costs must have added somewhat to the overheads of the business. The move to Ipswich in 1746, to a site beside the River Orwell right below the Holywells, from which the water could be piped into the brewery, made sense in every way.

Ipswich was a much larger town than Harwich, and although the Essex town was the packet port for the Low Countries, used by passengers travelling to many parts of Europe, the Suffolk county town undoubtedly offered Thomas Cobbold much better prospects. A number of breweries were already established in the town, but in his out-of-town situation adjacent to a supply of pure water Cobbold enjoyed an undoubted advantage over them all.

The town to which Thomas Cobbold transferred his business was already a thousand years old. Not that Thomas would have been impressed even had he known that Ipswich had been founded by the Wuffinga dynasty as a trading entrepot at a period when town life was virtually unknown in England.

For him the present, and the future, was what mattered, not the past. The wooden buildings of his new brewery were erected at a spot known to local people as The Cliff, a little over half a mile below

A view of Harwich from seaward showing the brewery just to the right of St Nicholas's Church. The move from this site to Ipswich in 1746 solved the brewery's water supply problem.

A water schuyt of the kind that Thomas Cobbold used to supply his Harwich brewery with sweet water from the Holy Wells at Ipswich, from a Dutch print of 1789.

the town quays at which small sailing ships unloaded their cargoes of coal and timber. Little ships they were, indeed, for the river had silted so much that the larger vessels had to lie at anchor downriver and their cargoes were carried up to the quays by lighters. Truth to tell, Ipswich was at the bottom of one of its periodic depressions, and Thomas might well have felt that the only way was upwards. He died in 1752, so he was to have no part in the regrowth of the town that occurred during the latter part of the 18th century, but his descendants were to play a most significant part in that regeneration.

Thomas's son, another Thomas, carried on the business until his own death on 21st April, 1767. He was buried in St Clement's Church, in the port area of Ipswich, and on the flagstone that marks his resting place he is described as a common brewer. There is no disrespect in that description, for a common brewer was simply a tradesman who brewed for the trade rather than someone who produced beer only for sale on the premises or for home consumption.

We know very little of the brewing trade at this time, but it is fairly certain that the younger Thomas had plenty of competition, with at least a dozen breweries operating in the town. Many taverns at that time had their own brewhouses, though one wonders what the quality of the product might have been. Certainly the science of brewing was less well understood then than it is today, and not all those who produced ale and beer at the back of the premises took as much care over the quality of their raw materials and over the brewing process as they might have done.

Ale or beer was the normal drink of the working man, with "small beer" for the children, for most of the water available in the poorer parts of a town such as Ipswich was grossly polluted; all too often the cesspool and the well were near neighbours. When the first Medical Officer of Health was appointed in Ipswich in the 1870s he reported in his first year that "Typhoid Fever has been prevalent throughout the whole year, principal causes being the air poisoned by foul emanations from drains and sewers and pollution of the drinking water". Whatever the views of the Temperance movement, the product of the brewing process was more wholesome than the well water.

The third generation, John Cobbold (1746-1835).

The younger Thomas had five children, born between 1742 and 1750. It was the third child, John, who carried on the family business, or rather businesses, and it was also he that built Holywells mansion in 1814 at the top of the hill overlooking the springs that had given rise to the brewery at the bottom.

One speaks of the family's commercial interests in the plural, for they by no means confined themselves to brewing. John was also a maltster, no doubt producing in his maltings in St Clement's Fore Street and at the Cliff much if not all of the malt which went into the mash tun at the brewery, and as a profitable sideline also dealt in coal and corn. With one of his sons he also set up a wine merchant's business which is still flourishing today under the name of Heyman Barwell Jones with Richard Cobbold as managing director.

The family also had shipping interests, owning a number of vessels which traded world-wide from Ipswich.

And when in 1825 the Blue Bank in Ipswich failed the Cobbolds went into banking, putting new capital into the business to save it from collapse. The bank had been founded by C.A. Crickitt, J. Kerridge and William Truelove in Tavern Street about 1786 in opposition to Alexander's bank, known as the Yellow Bank in reference to the politics of the Quaker Alexander family. With John Cobbold and his son both putting money into the business, along with Ipswich solicitor William Rodwell, the firm became Bacon, Cobbold, Rodwell, Duningham and Cobbold, the repetition of the Cobbold name indicating the presence of the two partners, father and son. On John Cobbold's death he was succeeded in the partnership by his grandson, John Patteson Cobbold.

The Cobbolds also became involved in the Harwich bank founded by Charles Cox about 1775, John Cobbold joining the firm in 1839, after which it was known as Cox, Cobbold & Company. It was absorbed in 1893 by Bacon, Cobbold, Tollemache & Company of Ipswich, which in 1904 was taken over by the Capital & Counties Bank and eventually became part of Lloyds Bank.

The Cobbold family and the town

2

THE SECOND half of the 18th century saw the beginnings of a revival in the fortunes of Ipswich that was to be continued throughout the 19th. In 1789 Robert Ransome set up a foundry in St Margaret's Ditches, a business that was to grow into one of the world's biggest producers of agricultural machinery; the following year William Churchman set up a manufacturing tobacconist's shop at Hyde Park Corner which was to develop into a widely-known business; and at the beginning of the 19th century there began the process by which Ipswich was to be turned into a modern port, the River Commissioners appointed in 1806 employing one of the very first steam dredgers to cut through the mudbanks that had prevented larger ships from reaching the town quays. The Cobbolds both benefited from and aided efforts to improve the situation of the town.

John's first wife, Elizabeth Wilkinson, died in 1790, leaving him with fourteen children. For his second wife he took Elizabeth Clarke, the young widow of William Clarke, controller of customs at Ipswich; she had been widowed only six months after the wedding. Twenty years his junior, she not only brought up the children of John's first marriage but herself became the mother of six sons and a daughter, yet she still found time to carry on a lively correspondence with members of the family, to write poetry, and to do much more besides.

To quote G.R. Clarke, the Ipswich historian, "Her genius, talents, and acquirements, were of a superior and varied description. As a poet, she was graceful, playful, or pathetic; and an easy elegance pervaded all the production of her pen. She was eminently skilled in music, drawing, botany, mineralogy, and conchology; well versed in the sciences, history and antiquities; and had also an extraordinary talent of cutting portraits, landscapes, &c. in paper, with facility and correctness. She was possessed also of another rare accomplishment for a female, — she was a powerful and persuasive orator. . ."

The new Mrs Cobbold quickly made the family home at The Cliff and for a period at the Manor House on St Margaret's Green something of a centre of local artistic life. She was one of the young John Constable's earliest supporters, and he frequently stayed with the family. There can be little doubt that it was from his mother that her fifth son Richard obtained his own literary leanings; he is remembered today both as a sympathetic country parson with a sense of humour and as a Victorian novelist.

It was while the family was living on St Margaret's Green that a

The Manor House on St Margaret's Green, which was for some years the Cobbold family home before John Cobbold built Holywells mansion in 1814.

certain Margaret Catchpole became a servant in the Cobbold household. A country woman, Margaret was clearly a strong-willed personality who had a nasty habit of getting herself into trouble.

The true story of Margaret is now almost inextricably confused with a tangled web of fiction. For Margaret became the heroine of the Rev Richard Cobbold's first and most successful novel; although in true Victorian fashion the parson-novelist began by testifying to the truth of all that was written, he embroidered the basic facts with a great deal of fiction. A generation after its first publication, Cobbold's novel was declared to be "the best read book in Ipswich, if not in Suffolk".

Margaret was not the wilful young girl with a smuggler lover that the parson-writer portrayed in the novel. At the time she stole John Cobbold's strawberry roan, a crime for which she was sentenced to death at Suffolk Assizes at Bury St Edmunds in 1797, she was a woman of thirty-five. She was, however, a very determined woman, for in 1800 she escaped from Ipswich Gaol "in the absence of the Keeper, who was attending his duty at Bury Assizes" by scaling the wall with a clothes line. Again the death sentence was passed, but it was commuted to transportation; it is said that Mrs Cobbold wrote pleading for her life.

In later life the Rev Richard Cobbold remembered being taken by his mother to visit Margaret in Ipswich Gaol, and his memories of those visits were sufficiently vivid to be thoroughly convincing. However, at the time Margaret Catchpole stole his father's horse and rode off to London, the cot was being prepared for Master

Richard, and he was still not four years old when Margaret left for Australia in the transport *Nile*, never to return.

Perhaps it was his sense of fun as much as his imagination that caused the Rev Richard to tell such stories. When in his sixties, he was fitted with a set of false teeth, quite a rarity in those days, and while out walking in his parish he came upon two chimneysweeps sitting munching their breakfast. He got into conversation with them, and while chatting said how much he envied their nice white teeth. Back came the quick retort that they would change teeth with him for a pound.

Richard Cobbold pretended to tug at his, and finally after a good deal of apparent effort pulled them out. Greatly alarmed, the two sweeps jumped up and rushed off to the nearby Queen's Head, where they cried to Mrs Mary Allen, the landlady, "Missus, give us some brandy — we've just seen the Devil!"

It was something more than a sense of humour, one suspects, that caused the Rev Richard to write to the *Suffolk Chronicle* in 1859 claiming that Margaret Catchpole was on a visit to Ipswich. "Yes, sir, she was in the train with me," he wrote with the straightest of faces. "Margaret Catchpole is upon a visit to Mr. Roe's in Brook Street in your town. . .Perhaps some who remember her may like to see her."

The public rose to the bait, and Owen Roe's shop at 2 Upper Brook Street, Ipswich, was besieged by the curious. All that the

A photograph of Cliff House taken in the latter part of the 19th century, when it was also a Cobbold residence.

crowds saw was a painting, highly imaginative, no doubt, of Margaret Catchpole by her "biographer".

It is unlikely that Mr Owen Roe, looking-glass manufacturer, carver, gilder and picture dealer, had ever had so many potential customers gathering outside his shop. Perhaps he thought what a good day it had been for him when his cousin, Ann Roe, had married Charles Cobbold, the Rev Richard's brother. Publicity stunts are nothing new.

Margaret Catchpole had in fact been dead for some years, for she had died out in New South Wales in 1819, having contracted an illness that proved fatal from a farmworker she was nursing.

It was typical of Mrs Elizabeth Cobbold that she carried on a correspondence with her former servant out in Botany Bay. Some of Margaret Catchpole's letters to Elizabeth are still preserved, very different from the much-edited "letters" reproduced in Richard's novel. One can almost hear Margaret's strong Suffolk accent as one reads:

> "Mrs Palmer was verry sorrey to partt with me she is a verry nices Laday and was very happey to find i had such a good frind as you my good Laday and said she niver read such a good Letter as that of Mrs Sleorgin and hoped that i would read it to her searvant and that she had a grat mind to had it put in to the newes paper and that yours was a very nices Letter in ded and said she had no dought But that i was wothey of all the favers that was showen to me for so grat a spirit and that i had Behaved my self so well . . .But if i Cold But onces return to my owen native Land what a happey woman shoud i Be But my good Laday it is you that giv me all the happiness that i have hear for i keep my self free from all men and that is more than any woman Can say in the hol Colony young or old for the young girles that are Born in this Countrey marry very young at 14 and 15 years old. . ."

John Cobbold's eldest son, also John, married Harriet Chevallier, a member of the family from Aspall that was later to give its name to Chevallier barley, a fine malting barley that had its origin in an ear that a labourer found in his boot after a day's threshing. No doubt much of it found its way into the Cobbold maltings.

The fourth generation, John Cobbold (1774-1860).

The fourth generation John was twenty-three when his eldest son John Chevallier Cobbold was born, in the same year that saw the birth of his uncle Richard. Earlier generations had played their part in the commercial life of Ipswich, but it was John Chevallier Cobbold who was to take the major role in the town's public life.

"I take this gentleman as one so closely mixed up with the social and public life of the town as to be inseparable from the actual identity of Ipswich," wrote the author of *Public Men of Ipswich and East Suffolk*, a series of personal sketches which appeared in the *Suffolk Mercury* in the 1870s. "Apart from politics and apart from differences of opinion of any kind, if a stranger were to ask me to pick out a native of the old borough to stand forward in some emblematical position to represent the town — just as the quaint old half-boats and queer, impossible amphibious animals represent Ipswich on the ancient arms of the borough — I should not hesitate to nominate Mr Cobbold.

"For 20 years he represented Ipswich in Parliament. In all that he did in the House of Commons he was more or less closely identified with the town. At home his Conservatism never for a moment stood in his way as a believer in progress. The local party of improvement might depend upon him as if he had been a Radical, and he is personally as intimately identified with new Ipswich as with old."

There were few, if any, other men in 19th-century Ipswich who deserved such commendation. There were few aspects of local affairs in which he was not involved, and the wisdom he displayed has been confirmed by hindsight. When a meeting was held at the Moot Hall in Ipswich in January, 1836, to consider a proposal for forming a Wet Dock and improving the river J.C. Cobbold was there, and he it was who was asked by William Lane to read the prospectus of a plan that he, Lane, had prepared.

When a committee was formed to collect information J.C. Cobbold was, unsurprisingly, one of the members. He later became one of the Dock Commissioners appointed under the Ipswich Dock Act of 1837, a piece of legislation that received Royal Assent just ten days after Queen Victoria's accession to the throne.

One of the Cobbold fleet, the barque John Cobbold, giving assistance to the Sunderland barque Derwent during a storm in the Atlantic in March, 1874. This spirited painting of the incident still hangs at Glemham Hall.

John Chevallier Cobbold (1797-1882), who was an Ipswich dock commissioner, was instrumental in bringing the railway to Ipswich, and represented the town of Ipswich in Parliament from 1847 to 1868. He served as High Steward of Ipswich from 1875 until his death.

It was appropriate that he should be Mayor of Ipswich in 1842, the year in which the dock was opened. The actual day of the opening, 17th January, was, as one of the local newspapers reported, "unfavourable for any public ceremony for such an occasion", but Cobbold boarded a little sloop, the *Director*, and sailed out through the new lock when she left for Rochester with a cargo of grain and general goods. It is not recorded where he left the *Director*, but one can be certain he did not sail in her to Rochester but came ashore at

A painting by Fred Russell of the old brewery, much of which dated from 1746. Little of this survived the building of the new brewery in 1894, but Cliff House on the left of the picture is now the Brewery Tap.

some much nearer wharf; perhaps he was put ashore close to the brewery at the Cliff.

The Cobbolds were also much involved in attempts to bring the railway to Suffolk. J.C. Cobbold and his father, John Cobbold, as well as John Cobbold's brother-in-law, the Rev. Dr John Chevallier, were prominent among the Suffolk supporters of the Grand Eastern Counties Railway, whose prospectus was issued in 1834; the intention of the company was to build a line from London to Yarmouth by way of Ipswich and Norwich.

When the Eastern Counties (having dropped the Grand from its title) ground to a halt at Colchester and the directors from the North began to wage a power struggle in which they forced out the Suffolk directors, J.C. Cobbold, finding himself outvoted in all his efforts to have the line continued beyond Colchester, decided that it would be necessary to promote a new company if the railway were to be brought to Ipswich. Thus was born the Eastern Union Railway, intended to unite Ipswich with Colchester, and so with London.

John Chevallier Cobbold, who was chairman throughout the life of the company, was later to say that he and his friends had originally subscribed a tenth of the capital of the Eastern Union Railway between them so that a Bill could be submitted to Parliament. As one of the two treasurers of the Ipswich and East Suffolk Hospital, he and his co-treasurer Dykes Alexander offered to advance the railway company £600 at five per cent interest "on receipt of a temporary

1639
Ye Olde NEPTVNE INNe

acknowledgement for such loan until the Directors were authorised to issue debenture bonds". As Hugh Moffat, historian of the early railways in East Anglia, puts it, a modern auditor would not consider this to be a suitable trustee investment!

The day of the official opening of the Eastern Union line was a public holiday in Ipswich. As the first passenger train left the station at the top of Croft Street at 10.30 am on 11th June, 1846, beneath a triumphal arch six hundred ladies in a specially erected grandstand waved "snowy kerchiefs" and a band on the train played God Save the Queen. John Chevallier Cobbold joined the train at the first stop, at Bentley. The festivities of that day ended with a balloon ascent and fireworks by the Wet Dock, but the effect of the coming of the railway would be felt for many years ahead as commerce and industry were stimulated by the new opportunities both for bringing in raw materials and for sending out products.

The two Cobbolds were later to become directors of the Ipswich and Bury St Edmunds Railway Company which extended the line to Bury, and within a few years had seen the line extended also to Norwich. The working of the Eastern Union was taken over in 1854 by its deadly rival, the Eastern Counties Railway, and in 1862 they both became part of the Great Eastern Railway. The line which owed so much to the Cobbolds is still remembered, however, for in Croft Street, not far from the original Ipswich station, there is the E.U.R. Tavern, formerly a Tolly Cobbold house.

The seaside resort of Felixstowe, which was eventually to be greatly developed by the Great Eastern Railway Company formed out of the Eastern Union, Eastern Counties and other East Anglian

Opposite page: The Old Neptune Inn, Fore Street, a former merchant's house dating from the 15th and 16th centuries which became an inn some time during the 18th century. It is now again a private house.

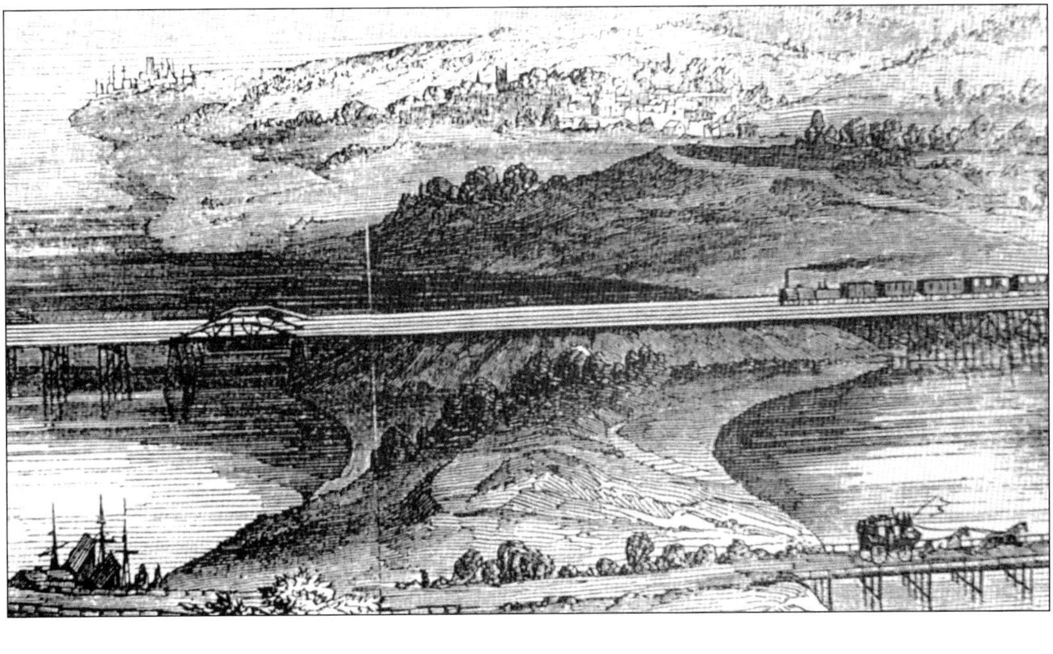

The timber viaducts carring the Eastern Union Railway over the Stour at Cattawade, as seen in a print of 1846. The coach in the foreground ceased running once the railway was in operation.

An advertisement for the Bath Hotel at Felixstowe dating from the latter part of the 19th century. Henry George Quilter came from Aston, Birmingham, to take over the Bath Hotel in the 1880s.

The original Fludyer Arms, built about 1833, was some forty years old when this photograph was taken by Charles Emeny. It took its name from the family from whom John Chevallier Cobbold bought his seaside residence.

One of the early houses built at Felixstowe on land bought by John Chevallier Cobbold from the Duke of Hamilton. The standpipe on the edge of the pavement is a survival from a scheme to supply water from springs in the cliff.

lines in 1862, was no more than an embryonic extension to the village of Walton when John Chevallier Cobbold built its first hotel in 1839. He was among the first Ipswich businessmen to settle in Felixstowe for the summer months when he took Felixstowe Cottage, an attractive seaside residence developed from a fisherman's cottage nestling under the cliff, from Sir Samuel Brudenell Fludyer, Bart. Later Cobbolds had the Fludyer's Arms, a wooden public house at the back of the beach which was replaced by a fine brick building early in the present century.

In the middle of the century John Chevallier Cobbold bought land at the Spa end of the growing town from the Duke of Hamilton, whose name was taken for the main thoroughfare, and began to develop the area. One of the roads to the east of Hamilton Road was named Cobbold Road in recognition of his part in promoting the growth of the new town, which by the turn of the century had a population of more than 4,000, eight times as many as when J.C. Cobbold spent his first summer there.

His lifetime of public service was recognised in 1875 when he was appointed High Steward of Ipswich, a position of honour which he occupied until his death in 1882.

John Patteson Cobbold (1831-1875) as Mayor of Ipswich in 1867. His brother, Felix Thornley Cobbold, was Mayor in 1896 and presented Christchurch Mansion, below, to the town.

His son, John Patteson Cobbold, followed in his footsteps, becoming Mayor of Ipswich in 1867 and MP for the borough in 1874, but he predeceased his father; a children's wing was added to the East Suffolk and Ipswich Hospital as a memorial to him.

Others of the family took up the political banner, however, Thomas Clement Cobbold entering Parliament in 1875 and Felix Thornley Cobbold following him to Westminster in 1885. The latter was, among many other things, vice-president of the Ipswich Swimming Club, and was instrumental in persuading Ipswich Town Council to construct the first indoor swimming pool in the town, Fore Street Baths, opened in 1894. He not only gave the land on which the baths were built but provided £1,200 towards the cost of the building, which was designed by T.W. Cotman, who designed a number of public houses for the Cobbolds.

At the opening he expressed the opinion that "there should be no differences between men in a bath". He remarked that in some towns there were different classes, the poor only being admitted at the end of the week when the water was dirty. Alas, the Corporation took no notice of his speech, and cards were hung outside the baths each day to show what classes were being admitted at the time.

Felix Thornley Cobbold was Mayor of Ipswich in 1896, the year after he had presented Christchurch Mansion to the town. He followed up this spectacular gift by giving the town Gippeswyk Park in 1910, and when he died he left a legacy of £20,000 to the town council for the purchase of pictures and works of art.

The 19th-century breweries 3

THROUGHOUT the 19th century the town of Ipswich was expanding at an even faster rate than other towns in Suffolk, leading both to a shortage of housing and to a rapid expansion of the built-up area. The opportunities for a brewing firm were plain to see.

At the time of the first Census, taken in 1801, the town's population was a mere 11,277. Most of those people were living in the area within the medieval town ditch and in the old parishes immediately outside, but by 1851 the population had almost trebled to 32,914 and new houses were being built on the outskirts of the town. Between 1831 and 1841 the number of houses increased from 4,116 to 5,240, and by 1851 another 1,739 had been built.

Catering for this growing population in mid-century were no fewer than fourteen brewers, though one of them was merely an agent for a Norwich brewery. Six of them were also licensed victuallers presumably producing beer for consumption on their own premises; among the hostelries which brewed their own beer were the Cock and Pye in Upper Brook Street, the Rose and Crown in Norwich Road, the Vine in Church Street, St Clement's, and the Tower Brewery Inn, which was in Northgate Street.

With the dawn of the 20th century the population had doubled again to 66,630, just about half the present-day figure. Elsewhere in Suffolk the population was also increasing, in spite of the influx of working people into Ipswich which resulted in such startling growth.

Ransomes alone employed upwards of 1,500 men and boys, rising at the beginning of the 20th century to some 2,500, and publicans in Duke Street prepared for the dinnertime break by drawing off pint after pint and lining them up on the counter in readiness for the influx of thirsty workers. Beer was the normal drink of the working man, and every one of those leaving Orwell Works dropped his pence on the bar and quaffed his pint on the way home to dinner.

Home for many of them was a tenement just off the Wash, aptly named since a stream flowed down the street from Spring Road, in wet weather overflowing and turning the whole street into a morass; at the Orwell Place junction there were stepping stones to enable people to get across.

As with so many other large towns, it is said that there was a time when Ipswich had a pub for every day of the year. That could be true, since in 1893 there were 308 licensed premises in the borough, and the temperance movement had already been actively campaigning for some years for a reduction in the number of licences granted by the Justices.

St Helen's, Ipswich, about 1910. In the left foreground is the Grove Tavern, and in the distance just behind the tram is the Dove Inn; between them is the Water Lily.

The story is told of how the residents of St. Helen's, that little hamlet that had grown up outside the ramparts at a very early stage in the town's history, challenged all comers to drink a pint at each hostelry from the Grove Tavern to the Salutation in Carr Street. Nobody who took up the challenge ever managed to reach the Salutation.

Even if the challenger resisted the temptation to have a second or a third glass in any one pub, and no doubt the locals made sure that the temptation was overwhelming, he would still be one over the eight before getting to the Salutation. After the Grove Tavern came the Water Lily, then the Brickmaker's Arms, the Dove and the Olive Leaf, the May Bush, then the County Hotel on the corner of Orchard Street, the Mitre, the Beehive, that's nine pints, and only then did one come to the Salutation.

Perhaps the oddest of the town's many public houses in the 1840s was the Sunk Light Inn, situated between the Cliff Brewery and Greenwich Farm, whose fields have now disappeared under the dock installations of Cliff Quay. The Sunk Light Inn was an old vessel lying in a mud berth at right angles to the shore and reached by a staging and a set of steps; possibly it was indeed the former Sunk lightship, marking the entrance to the East Swin some twelve nautical miles off Harwich. It is not recorded whether or not this was a Cobbold "house".

Some of the Cobbold houses in Ipswich were buildings of considerable antiquity which had begun their lives as the homes of well-to-do merchants in the days when Ipswich traded in French

The old brewery seen in a photograph probably taken about 1880.

wine and Icelandic cod, English woollen cloth and much else besides. Perhaps the best known of these was the Neptune Inn, an interesting example of a hall house partly of 15th-century date which had been modernised in 1639.

When the licence was transferred in 1937 the Old Neptune, as it was then called, had been an inn for some two centuries. Its history is somewhat obscure, but in 1777 when the property was leased by Thomas Moore to Daniel Orford it was said to be "lately called Neptune Inn". It probably came into the hands of John Cobbold after the death in 1845 of the Quaker banker Dykes Alexander, who had come into possession of the property some 30 years earlier. Some of the panelling from the Neptune Inn found its way into the dining room at Holywells.

Another such old house was the Ram Inn, which stood in Key Street not far from the Common Quay. It was reputedly the birthplace of the great 16th-century merchant Henry Tooley. When it was demolished John Dupuis Cobbold, Mayor of Ipswich in 1915, presented to Christchurch Mansion the old corner post bearing the merchant's mark of its original owner.

Some dark deeds have been committed in certain of the town's hostelries. One Cobbold public house, the Swan Inn, which stands in King Street opposite the entrance to the Corn Exchange, was reputedly the scene of a murder in the dimly remembered past, as a result of which a perpetual fine of two pounds per annum was imposed. In fact the payment of two pounds, still made each year to the churchwardens of St Mary-le-Tower, dates back no further than

The Halberd Inn is on the site of the North Gate of Ipswich, demolished in 1794. The name of the narrow street beside it, Tower Ramparts, refers to the old town bank in the vicinity of St Mary-le-Tower Church.

1664 when John Parker "gave Forty Shillings a Year, to be paid out of the Swan Inn in this Parish, to buy Coals for the Poor", according to *An Account of the Gifts and Legacies that Have been given and bequeathed to Charitable Uses in the Town of Ipswich* published in 1747. There is no mention of when the coal was supplied, though under another similar charity established by William Neave, one of the Portmen of the town, the coal was to be distributed on St Thomas's Day, 21st December.

It has to be admitted that some of the town's 308 public houses were by no means bright and spacious, and many of them were probably downright insalubrious. Take the Blue Anchor in Lower Orwell Street, better known as the Lower Wash; it had only a small bar and just one other small room available to customers, though the licensee's parlour was also sometimes used by favoured customers even if it was the only living room for the tenant and his family.

Small wonder that about 1912 the magistrates recommended that the Blue Anchor should be closed. Besides the Gun at the bottom of Lower Orwell Street, on the corner of Key Street, and the Bull's Head at the top there were no fewer than sixteen other licensed premises within a radius of 200 yards of the Blue Anchor — and that in spite of the fact that seven licences had already been taken away in the neighbourhood.

Yet the brewers were able to refute any suggestion that the Blue

Anchor did not really do enough trade for it to pay. One man had been tenant for twelve years, and then left only because of domestic trouble; during his time there he had been able to save £500. When he left his son-in-law took over, and only when he died did a new tenant take the premises. All three had paid their rents and their accounts regularly and punctually, according to the brewers.

Perhaps the licensee's income did not depend on beer alone, for the sitting tenant raised a laugh in the magistrates' court when he told the justices that he "sold several things, including pickled onions".

Owners of the Blue Anchor were Catchpole & Co., of the Unicorn Brewery at the top of Foundation Street. At the time the licensing justices were considering whether or not to renew the licence of the Blue Anchor they were just one of half a dozen or so brewers with premises in Ipswich; even one of the Norwich companies had a depot in the cattle market area.

The third brewing company actually brewing in Ipswich was Tollemache's Ipswich Brewery Ltd, operating from the "steam brewery" in Upper Brook Street which had been opened by Charles Cullingham & Co. in 1856. Standing on land which had once been gardens and is now the Tacket Street car park, this brewery was at the time of its building the most up-to-date in Ipswich, equipped with the very latest in brewing technology.

A Victorian photograph of Helmingham Hall, the home of the Tollemache family for some 500 years. Queen Elizabeth I stayed there on two occasions.

The Felix Hotel at Felixstowe was designed by the Hon. Douglas Tollemache and architect T.W. Cotman, and opened in 1903. The photograph above shows one of the side gates of the hotel, which is now known as Harvest House.

The Tollemaches are an old-established Suffolk family who held the manor of Bentley, south of Ipswich; the couplet "Before the Normans into England came, Bentley was my seat and Tollemache was my name" is reputed to have been inscribed on the old manor house at Bentley. Nonetheless, it is fairly certain that the family originated in Normandy, even if they did precede William in emigrating to England. They later acquired Helmingham Hall, now the home of the present Lord Tollemache, through the marriage in 1487 of John Tollemache and Elizabeth Joyce; their son also married a Joyce, and Helmingham then became the principal Tollemache property, Bentley being henceforth the younger son's estate. It was through a later marriage that Peckforton, in Cheshire, came into the possession of the Tollemaches; the present Peckforton Castle was designed by Anthony Salvin, a pupil of John Nash, who was also involved in alterations to Helmingham Hall and the restoration of Helmingham Church. Queen Elizabeth I reputedly stayed at Helmingham Hall twice, the first time in 1561 and then again some twenty years later, and left behind her lute. During the Commonwealth period Helmingham was a headquarters of the original Society of the Sealed Knot, a Royalist secret organisation which played a leading part in restoring King Charles II to the throne.

John Tollemache, who in 1876 was created first Baron

Tollemache of Helmingham for services to agriculture, was one of John Chevallier Cobbold's fellow Members of Parliament. It was his sons, Douglas, Stanhope and Mortimer, who bought the Cullingham brewery in 1888.

The Hon. Douglas Tollemache, whose talent for business and hard work was largely responsible for the success of the brewing enterprise, joined the Bacon, Cobbold & Company bank in 1885. The Cobbold and Tollemache names were thus joined in the bank title well over half a century before the two brewery companies amalgamated to form Tollemache & Cobbold Breweries Ltd.

The Hon. Douglas Tollemache, who with his two brothers acquired the Cullingham brewery at Ipswich in 1888.

Having something more than just business acumen, the Hon. Douglas Tollemache collaborated with architect T.W. Cotman in designing the Felix Hotel at Felixstowe, opened in 1903. The largest and most magnificent of the growing resort's hotels, the Felix boasted not only 250 bedrooms but also twenty grass tennis courts, eight hard courts, two full-size croquet lawns and an 18-hole putting course.

Its splendid appearance on the cliff top contrasts with the relative seclusion of the Bath Hotel built in 1839 by John Chevallier Cobbold using bricks from a demolished martello tower. The Bath Hotel was destroyed in 1914, the victim of an arson attack by two Suffragettes, but the Felix Hotel survives, now converted into luxury flats.

T.W. Cotman, a nephew of John Sell Cotman, the Norwich School artist, designed a number of buildings for the Tollemaches, including the Crown & Anchor Hotel in Westgate Street, Ipswich, and also did a good deal of work for members of the Cobbold family. It is thought that the brewery foreman's house at Cliff Brewery, now the offices of Tollemache & Cobbold, which he designed for John Patteson Cobbold in 1869, was probably his first building.

In the course of a career spanning more than forty years he was responsible for the design of a number of Cobbold public houses in Ipswich, including The Gun in Key Street (1875), the Gardeners' Arms, Fore Hamlet (1879), the Royal Oak in Felixstowe Road (1882), the Cross Keys in Carr Street (1888), the Lion's Head, Cauldwell Hall Road (1901), and the Duke of Kent in Upper Orwell Street (1903), as well as the White Horse Inn, Ferry Road, Felixstowe (also 1903).

When it came to building a new brewery in 1894–96, however, Cobbolds sought a specialist architect who was closely associated with the brewing industry. The new Cliff Brewery was designed by William Bradford, senior partner of a London firm of architects and consulting engineers, who had a decade earlier been responsible for the Unicorn Brewery near the top of Foundation Street, built by Ipswich builders J.B. & F. Bennett for Catchpole & Co.

Cobbolds did not bring in any of the local builders, but instead employed their own building workmen to erect the new brewery, which embodied all the latest principles. It had a horizontal steam engine produced by the Ipswich engineering firm of E.R. & F. Turner, whose St Peter's Iron Works was situated between College

Street and the river. Still in working order, this engine stands today as a fine example both of Victorian technology and of Ipswich engineering.

Nevertheless, the brewery soon proved inadequate to the needs of the company, and in 1904 it had to be extended. Through all these changes care was taken to retain something of the former breweries; there is still to be seen a copper which was installed in the Harwich brewery back in 1723, and was moved to Ipswich in 1746.

Though the story of the Cliff Brewery might go back a mere 250 years, the tradition of brewing goes back much further.

Part of the old Cliff Brewery which survived for a time when the new brewery was built in 1894-96. It was, however, demolished in 1901 to make way for extensions to the new brewery.

Into the 20th century 4

THROUGHOUT the first half of the 20th century the two breweries, Tollemache's and Cobbold's, went their separate ways. At the beginning of 1923, a year during which Cobbold & Company celebrated their bicentenary with a big gathering in Holywells Park, there were more than 200 Cobbold licensed properties spread throughout Suffolk and North Essex.

Some of the buildings which belonged to Cobbold's at that time are still licensed, others still exist but are no longer public houses. The 17th-century Bull Inn at Brantham is still a meeting place for people from the old part of the village and is attracting customers from a much wider area, especially since one of the stars of the television series "It Ain't Half Hot Mum" took over the licence, but the equally old King's Head Hotel in Ipswich Street, Stowmarket, was demolished in the 1960s. The Grape Vine Inn at Mistley still stands right behind the famous swan fountain, but it is no longer licensed; nor is the Shoulder of Mutton Inn at Hadleigh, which was for a good many years a well-known antiques shop.

One which has disappeared altogether is the Lifeboat Inn at Shingle Street, that curious hamlet at the mouth of the River Ore. This public house was destroyed during the Second World War, when mysterious bombing experiments were carried out after the population had been evacuated. Just what happened there in wartime has never been revealed, but there has for years been plenty of speculation.

Felixstowe was always strongly Cobbold territory, not surprisingly since John Chevallier Cobbold owned so much land in the northern part of the town. When the Fludyer Arms was built at the back of the beach about 1833 it formed part of a very new seaside resort; only a few years earlier a visitor had reported that there were "many temporary stables just above the beach, for occasional parties who come in considerable numbers from the county around to dine & spend the day: when I was here about 3 years ago, I recollect but two of these booths, & I now found a large addition to them . . . The place seems to be in a very thriving condition many new houses have been built, & it promises ere long to become the fashionable resort of those who have money to throw away, & who cannot be satisfied with the comfort which they find in their own houses."

The Fludyer Arms (it was later known as The Fludyer's Arms, and then The Fludyers) took its name from Sir Samuel Brudenell Fludyer, Bart., who had had a residence nearby; he died in 1833. The original Fludyer Arms was a white-painted weatherboarded building which, as the sea ate away at the beach, finished up uncomfortably

The new Fludyer Hotel had not long replaced the wooden Fludyer's Arms when this advertisement appeared in Knight's Suffolk County Handbook of 1904. As a result of the patronage of the Empress of Germany, one of Queen Victoria's daughters, who spent the summer at Felixstowe with her children in 1891 the town was becoming an increasingly fashionable resort.

close to the water. It was replaced in 1903 by a new brick building on Undercliff Road East designed by A.H. Lambert, who became the brewery surveyor in 1899.

Cobbold's also owned the Ordnance Arms Hotel, where George Tomline took his guests to celebrate the opening in 1877 of the Felixstowe Railway; they had travelled from Westerfield to the old pier on Harwich Harbour behind an engine named Tomline, with George Tomline himself on the footplate, and had then been taken up to the hotel on his two-foot gauge tramway, which terminated more or less on the site of the Felixstowe Leisure Centre. Built by John Cobbold in 1854, it seems often to have been referred to simply as "the Ordnance", or even "the Ordinance", and after being enlarged in 1914 it officially dropped the word Arms from its title.

A ticket entitling the holder to a free pint issued in connection with the bicentenary celebrations in 1923.

In Ipswich itself the Cobbold houses included the Bull Inn, one of the dock area pubs. Although it dates from the 16th century and was rated in 1689 at £40 per annum, £5 per annum more than the White Horse in Tavern Street, it had been given a brick front to disguise its timber framing some time at the beginning of the 19th century. It was due to be demolished in the 1970s, but after pleas from conservationists was reprieved and turned to commercial use.

Less fortunate was an early 16th-century house in Carr Street, probably built as the residence of an affluent merchant or tradesman, which became an inn during the 17th century. As the Cross Keys it is said to have become an important coaching house,

The Bull in Key Street, Ipswich, had closed by the time this photograph was taken about 1979. During the First World War a Zeppelin bomb fell close by, killing a man and demolishing a next-door cottage.

with an extensive range of stables at the rear, but the main coaching inns were the Great White Horse, the White Hart in St Lawrence Street and the Suffolk Hotel in Westgate Street. At one period the Cross Keys actually gave its name to the street in which it was situated, but when Carr Street was widened about 1888 the old inn was demolished, to be replaced by an imposing brick building designed by T.M. Cotman. That in turn disappeared when the Carr Street Precinct was developed in the 1970s.

So prolific were Cobbold pubs in Ipswich that *Punch*, that doyen of English humour, once published an excruciating pun (one hesitates to call it a joke):

Q: Why is Ipswich like an old shoe?
A: Because it is 'Cobbold' all over.

Holywells Park was the setting for a celebration on 30th July, 1923, of the bicentenary of the company. Felix Walton, whose name

Festivities at Holywells to mark the bicentenary of the Cobbold brewery included barrel rolling races. In later years the chairman of Tolly Cobbold, the Hon Peter Strutt, was to recall that one of the skills he learnt during his early days at the Tollemache brewery in Upper Brook Street was rolling barrels across the brewery yard.

was by no means unfamiliar to readers of the local newspapers, wrote a short history of the Cliff Brewery in which he also surveyed the public service of the Cobbold family, which had by then supplied five Mayors of Ipswich and four Members of Parliament.

In the year of the Cobbold & Company bicentenary Catchpole's Unicorn Brewery closed, and Cobbold's and the Tollemaches shared the Catchpole public houses between them. The story is told that the pubs were allocated between the two firms by the toss of a coin, a distinctly friendly and effective method of decision making. That raised the number of Cobbold houses to some 270.

The following year Cobbold & Company and the wine and spirit business which had for many years been carried on by Cobbold & Sons were brought together as Cobbold & Co. Ltd. John Dupuis Cobbold (who had been running the brewery in partnership with his brother, Philip Wyndham Cobbold) became chairman of the new company, and his son, John Murray Cobbold, always known as Ivan, was appointed to the board of directors; he took over as chairman on his father's death in 1929.

Cliff Brewery from the air. Only a road and rail tracks separate the brewery from the Orwell, and it is easy to see from this view why later development and expansion left the Victorian brewery unobscured. EADT

IPSWICH
TOWN

The founding of Ipswich Town FC 5

BREWING WAS not Ivan Cobbold's only interest, however; he was a keen follower of football, and was president of Ipswich Town Football Club in the days when it was an amateur club. He more than anyone was responsible for the decision to bring professional football to Ipswich in 1936.

The old club had been unwilling to turn professional, and it had been decided to form an Ipswich United to field a professional team, but Ivan Cobbold's letter that appeared in the Evening Star on 24th April, 1936, settled the matter. He expressed himself firmly in favour of having a professional club, and a week later Ipswich Town and the proposed Ipswich United amalgamated to form a new Ipswich Town Football Club Ltd., with Ivan Cobbold as chairman.

Within the month the board had appointed the first manager, Mike O'Brien, who in a remarkably short time built up a side that was destined to put Ipswich on the footballing map by winning the Southern League Championship at its first attempt. And only two years after its formation the new professional club was elected to the Third Division South, thanks not only to the sound foundation laid by Mike O'Brien but also to the work of Scott Duncan, a former international who succeeded him as manager late in 1937.

Ivan Cobbold.

Ivan Cobbold, too, had played a leading part in gaining this success for the club. Along with the manager and another director he had undertaken a country-wide tour to canvass support in advance of the election meeting.

In the international field events were moving steadily towards war, and little more than a year after Ipswich Town's election to the League Britain was at war. Ivan Cobbold, who had been wounded during the First World War while serving with the Scots Guards, returned to his regiment; he was attached to the War Office with the rank of lieutenant-colonel, and was killed when a V1 flying bomb destroyed the Guards Chapel in Wellington Barracks during a service on Sunday, 18th June, 1944. Major Robert Cobbold, Philip Wyndham Cobbold's elder son, had died at Cassino during the Italian campaign.

Philip Wyndham Cobbold filled the breach as chairman of the brewery company, and Ivan Cobbold's widow, Lady Blanche Cobbold, joined the board; she remained an active director until the amalgamation with Tollemache's in 1957. The new chairman died after little more than a year in office, and it fell to his son, Alistair Cobbold, to take up the reins of office. Alistair had been appointed to the board only in 1944 while serving in the Royal Navy Volunteer Reserve; he was for some time in command of the

Opposite page:
John Cobbold wearing his Ipswich Town shirt. Although he had as little as possible to do with the club, he was proud to be photographed in the club's blue jersey.

American-built Captain class frigate HMS *Inglis*, one of the vessels handed over to Britain under Lease-Lend.

Although he came to the post without much time to accustom himself to the brewing business, Alistair proved highly successful as company chairman. He served for more than ten years before handing over to John Cavendish Cobbold, the elder son of Lady Blanche Cobbold, in 1957.

John and his brother Patrick were as keen on football as their father had been, and both became well known at Portman Road, the Ipswich Town ground. John joined the board of the club in 1948 at the age of twenty-one and went on to become the club chairman, one of the youngest chairmen in the Football League. With his unstinted support the team went on to achieve great things. John once told *East Anglian Daily Times* sports editor Alan Everett that he would not cross the road to watch a football match unless Ipswich Town were playing, and Patrick professed to know little about football, but it is generally accepted that they both knew a good deal more than they acknowledged.

Patrick and John Cobbold at Portman Road with Bobby Robson at the time he took over as Ipswich Town's manager in the middle of the 1968-69 season. EADT

Patrick Cobbold receiving a testimonial marking Ipswich Town's centenary from Mr Arthur McMullen, vice-president of the Football Association, in 1987.

The amiable Scott Duncan, still remembered for his dark blue suit and black Homburg hat, came to the end of his long run as Town manager in 1955, having taken the club up to the Second Division and established them firmly in the Football League. He handed over to a former Tottenham Hotspur and England full-back with absolutely no managerial experience named Alf Ramsey, who was some years later to be knighted for his successful work as England manager after the national team had won the World Cup.

Under Alf Ramsey and John Cobbold Ipswich Town took the football world by storm, culminating in scenes of jubilation at Portman Road on 28th April, 1962, when Ipswich beat Aston Villa 2–0 to win the First Division championship at their first attempt. It was the first time a team had won the First Division title at the first attempt since Preston North End had done so in 1888–89, the year the Football League was founded.

Although he took a great interest in the game, John Cobbold had as little as possible to do with the footballing side of the club. It was his contention that the chairman's job was to appoint a manager, and then to let him get on with the job without undue interference. His view was that the chairman was responsible for the image of the club, and during his chairmanship Ipswich Town's hospitality became legendary across Europe.

When Bobby Robson took over as manager in the middle of the 1968–69 season he spent his first three years at Ipswich fighting against relegation. At the beginning of the 1971 season the supporters turned against him and there were chants of "Robson out!", but he retained the backing of John Cobbold and the board. An outraged John commented "I've never heard anything like it at Portman Road before."

Opposite page: As chairman Patrick Cobbold had the job of signing the many Christmas cards sent out by Ipswich Town Football Club. His chairmanship of the club was something he took very seriously. EADT

Years later Bobby Robson recalled how John Cobbold "could turn disappointment and disaster into laughter — there was always tomorrow as far as Mr. John was concerned".

John stepped down as chairman in 1976, and was succeeded by his younger brother Patrick. It was during Patrick's chairmanship that Ipswich Town reached its greatest heights, beating Arsenal at Wembley on 6th May, 1978, to take the Football Association Cup. Lady Blanche, as the club president, and her two sons were at Wembley to see their team triumph over a side that was described in the match programme as "not so much a football club, more an institution".

It is said that at the end of the match Lady Blanche was asked if she would like to meet Margaret Thatcher, then Prime Minister. "I'd rather have another gin and tonic," was her reply.

The Cobbolds later led the celebrations in Ipswich, where the team rode through the town in an open-top bus, captain Mick Mills holding aloft the prized FA Cup. A man of great emotions, John unashamedly shed tears of joy.

In 1981 Ipswich Town followed up their FA Cup success by

John and Patrick Cobbold pose joyfully with the FA Cup, won by Ipswich Town in 1978. Patrick had taken over the chairmanship from his brother two years earlier. EADT

winning the UEFA Cup, a triumph in European football that gave the Cobbolds further cause for celebration.

In later days Patrick Cobbold accompanied the Ipswich Town team on a pre-season tour which took them to Kiev, then a provincial capital in the Union of Soviet Socialist Republics. It entailed the kind of formal occasion which Patrick did not entirely relish when he was due to meet a top Communist official, who strode in grim-faced with his equally grim-faced bodyguard. With out-stretched hand, Patrick greeted him with "Do you know, I'm the nephew of Harold Macmillan?" It was a throwaway remark that broke the ice; there were smiles all round, and soon the vodka was flowing well.

It was, of course, quite true. Lady Blanche was a daughter of the Duke of Devonshire; her sister Dorothy had married the publisher and former Prime Minister.

Lady Blanche Cobbold, who was president of Ipswich Town Football Club

A friendly union 6

THE YEAR in which Alistair Cobbold handed over to John, 1957, was also the year of the amalgamation of Cobbold & Co. Ltd. and Tollemache's Breweries Ltd. Unlike some commercial arrangements which are well described as "hostile bids", this was an entirely amicable union of two old-established family firms which had for long been on friendly terms.

Indeed, to indicate that the merger was a partnership of equals it was agreed that the first chairman should be neither a Cobbold nor a Tollemache. So it was that Sir Thomas Bland, deputy chairman of Barclays Bank and High Sheriff of Suffolk in 1952, became chairman of Tollemache & Cobbold; he had succeeded Lord Belper, a son-in-law of the Hon. Douglas Tollemache, as chairman of the Tollemache brewery in 1954 and had initiated the discussions leading to the amalgamation.

With the amalgamation it made sense for the production process to be concentrated on one site, and a three-year enlargement of the Cliff Brewery began two years later. Production at the Tollemache brewery off Upper Brook Street came to an end in 1961 and the buildings were demolished; much of the site is now a car park.

Tollemaches had in 1920 bought the Essex Brewery at Walthamstow from Collier Brothers, and in 1934 had acquired a controlling interest in the Star Brewery at Cambridge, which became a wholly owned subsidiary in 1947. Even after brewing ceased at Walthamstow the brewery there continued to be used as a bottling depot until 1973, when a new bottling line was installed at the Cliff Brewery at a cost of some £140,000. Brewing had ceased at the Star Brewery at Cambridge the previous year, bringing to an end many centuries of brewing in the university town. At about the same time a new kegging line was installed at Ipswich to meet the rising demand for the company's keg beers.

Besides embarking on redevelopment costing a total of a quarter of a million pounds, the firm decided to give itself a new corporate image.

Out would go the statue of Bacchante, a naked lady holding a baby in one hand and a bunch of grapes in the other, which had been used on Tollemache labels since the 1920s. The actual statue had been brought back from Paris by the Hon Douglas Tollemache at the beginning of the century. And out would go the Cardinal Wolsey symbol which had been used by Cobbolds for many years.

"Brewers sack the nude and cardinal" was the headline that appeared in the *Daily Mail* on 12th April that year.

The new image was simpler and, as a company statement made

The old Cobbold trade mark, showing the Tudor gateway of Wolsey's college in College Street, Ipswich.

The Upper Brook Street brewery of Tollemache's Breweries Ltd. as seen by artist W.A. Southon. The original watercolour was presented to R.J. Scully, who was Tollemache's head brewer from 1926 to 1959; it now hangs in the Brewery Tap.

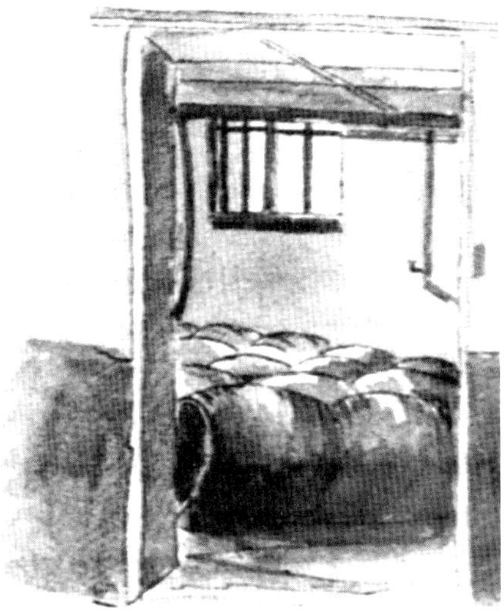

plain, less fragmented. The words "Tolly Cobbold" in a bold modern type face, coloured in shades of red and blue, took the place of Bacchante and Cardinal Wolsey on the bottle labels; everything from letterheads to drip mats and even the livery of the brewery drays was redesigned.

The year 1973 saw the celebration of the 250th anniversary of the opening by Thomas Cobbold of the Harwich brewery and the publication of a history of the firm written by Michael Jacobson. To mark the anniversary the Duke and Duchess of Kent paid a visit to the brewery, landing in a helicopter of the Queen's Flight on a nearby playing field and lunching in a marquee with members of the Tolly Cobbold staff.

A cricket match between a Tolly Cobbold XI and a Suffolk XI

Below: John Cobbold holds an umbrella over the Duchess of Kent as she and the Duke, on right, tour the brewery during their visit in 1973. EADT

was played to celebrate the anniversary, and a number of trophies were presented by Tolly Cobbold to various sports organisations to be competed for in future years.

"Today, Tolly Cobbold is one of the relatively few independent breweries remaining outside the major groups," said the *Morning Advertiser* in an article announcing the 1973 development plan. Not long afterwards the same paper contained news of a resolution adopted by the Ipswich Labour Party condemning "attempts by large brewing organisations to eradicate small brewing concerns and freehold public houses".

Although Tollemache & Cobbold more than once declared their intention of preserving the company's independence, the writing was on the wall. Great emphasis was laid on the firm's intention to remain independent when, towards the end of 1973, it was announced that Lord Tollemache, who had become chairman two years before, was resigning on his doctor's advice and that his successor was Eric Butler, who was also a director of Bass Charrington.

The 250th anniversary year was certainly a time of celebration, but there was little to cheer about when the year's trading results were announced. Caught in a vicious trap of higher overheads and frozen prices, Tolly Cobbold found its pre-tax profits down by a quarter. Difficulties with the new plant, which had prevented the brewery from meeting demand at the height of the summer season, compounded the problems posed by an adverse economic climate.

"If a takeover bid for this 250-year-old group should materialise, the founding families, with the help of Bass, should be in a position to stave off any attacker," said the *Morning Advertiser's* Richard Brent.

Three years later the threat materialised. Northern Foods, an aggressive and ambitious group which embraced North Country Breweries, was reported to have picked up an 11.8 per cent share stake in Tolly Cobbold and, as speculation mounted that a bid battle might soon break out, Tolly Cobbold shares increased in value. "Takeover talk is purely a speculators' invention," said John Cobbold towards the end of 1976 as the Tolly Cobbold share price soared.

While the financial world puzzled over the future of the firm, Tolly Cobbold collaborated with Eastern Arts in sponsoring a major national art exhibition. Uniquely, it was announced that up to half the £5,000 prize money could be taken in wines from their subsidiary Barwell & Jones. More than 1,400 entries were received, and the panel of judges had the task of selecting fifty-seven works for exhibition. This exhibition continued until 1987 and became something of an institution in the art world, with showings at the Royal Academy and other leading galleries throughout the country.

With a workforce that was traditionally extremely loyal to the company and on first-name terms with the management the Cliff Brewery saw little of the industrial unrest that afflicted so much of British industry in the sixties and seventies. Old employees speak of

A reproduction of the statue of Bacchante, the bronze statue which featured on the label of Tollemache's ales. A bacchante was a priestess who took part in festivals in honour of Bacchus, the god of wine and fertility.

Holiday camp owners and others from Clacton, Frinton and Walton-on-the-Naze being shown around Cliff Brewery by Lord Tollemache in 1970. He is pointing out that at the time the poster on the wall was printed mild ale cost a penny three-farthings a pint, less than one decimal penny. EADT

having day-to-day conversations not with "The Guv'nor" or "Mr Cobbold" but with "Mr John" or "Mr Patrick".

Just after the August Bank Holiday of 1977, however, dissatisfaction at take-home pay of less than £40 a week and what they claimed were delays in negotiations with the management led some 250 workers at the brewery to walk out on unofficial strike. They asked for a 100 per cent increase in their basic pay, and public houses in the Ipswich area and elsewhere quickly ran out of draught beer as the Ipswich strikers were joined by workers at the Cambridge, Colchester and Norwich distribution depots.

Managing director the Hon. Peter Strutt made an overnight trip by train back from his holiday in Scotland to discuss the matter with his fellow directors. John Cobbold, who was never averse to cracking jokes against himself, told afterwards how he was stopped by pickets outside the brewery gates; when they saw it was him they told him "Oh, it's you, Mr John! You can go in, you do bugger all anyway!"

The government of the day had set strict guidelines for pay awards, and there were some fears that the settlement that brought the strike to an end after a little less than a week exceeded those guidelines. A £7 increase on basic pay was granted, together with consolidation of threshold payments which meant a further increase on the basic pay. At the same time the management promised to review the annual bonus scheme and to review differentials within the works, but a claim for a cut in working hours to 35 hours a week was deemed impracticable at the time.

No sooner was the strike settled than there came the announcement that Tollemache & Cobbold Breweries Ltd. had been taken over by the Ellerman shipping group. After more than two centuries the Ipswich brewery had lost its independence.

Under new colours 7

WITH THE takeover by the Ellerman group, whose chief interests had hitherto been in shipping, travel and transport, Eric Butler handed over as chairman to Peter Laister, managing director of Ellerman Lines Ltd. and a director of Hartlepool brewers J.W. Cameron, acquired by Ellermans in 1975. Tolly Cobbold managing director the Hon. Peter Strutt joined the board of Ellerman Lines.

Those "in the know" suggested that the takeover had been to some extent engineered by Bass as a means of preventing Northern Foods from expanding into the brewery business.

For the shipping group it was a return to its earliest days; the founder of the Ellerman empire, Sir John Ellerman, a frequent visitor to the Felix Hotel at Felixstowe, is said to have controlled a number of breweries around the world at the beginning of the century. His son sold off many of the brewery holdings and concentrated on shipping, which by the 1970s was suffering a cruel and debilitating recession. It was the group's newly acquired brewing interests which alone avoided profits falling, as one writer with a taste for puns put it, "below the plimsoll line".

The takeover cost the new owners some £5.7 million, which some commentators thought to be a bargain price. With the deal went Tolly Cobbold's 360 public houses in Suffolk, north Essex, Norfolk and Cambridgeshire, to be added to the 750 houses Ellermans had acquired when they bought Cameron's. The acquisition made Ellerman Britain's eighth biggest pub-owner, and there were immediate fears that the trickle of pub closures in East Anglia would become a flood.

In spite of the changes the Cobbold family involvement in the brewery continued, and it was managing director the Hon. Peter Strutt who pulled the first pint to open a new Tolly Cobbold public house, the Dragonfly, at Orton Malborne, part of the expanding city of Peterborough, in June, 1978. The Dragonfly quickly proved all too popular as traditional ale drinkers flocked to it to enjoy the Ipswich brew, and in the first weeks of opening a number of special deliveries were needed to keep up with the demand.

A government announcement early in 1978 of a plan for about a thousand public houses to change hands so as to bring increased competition between brewers had been pre-empted a year earlier by an exchange between Tolly Cobbold and Trumans, by which Trumans acquired six Tolly Cobbold houses in Ipswich and the Ipswich brewers took over seven former Truman pubs in Colchester and North-east Essex.

The English pub was changing. There had been a time when the tenant of a little country pub would draw a customer's pint from a barrel set up under the bar, or better still from a barrel set up in the cellar; even as late as 1980 Fred Boggis, then 86, at the Admiral's Head at Little Bealings was still serving his beer from the barrel in the age-old way, but most public houses by that time had more modern ways of filling the glass.

Over the years Tolly Cobbold spent considerable sums on improving its public houses, and as time went on landlords were encouraged to serve food as well as drinks. This was a trend that necessitated many other changes, for kitchens had to be updated and in many cases it was necessary to set aside part of the building as a dining area, or even to build on a new dining room.

When a £5 million investment was announced at the beginning of 1979 less than half this sum was to be spent on the brewery. As much as £1.7 million was earmarked for improving existing public houses and building new ones. One of the older pubs that benefited was the Swan in King Street, Ipswich, an ancient timber-framed house on which the company spent some £100,000. The plaster front bears the date 1707, the year in which the Act of Union united the English and Scots Parliaments, but for the Swan this was no

Group Captain Sir Douglas Bader himself opened the Douglas Bader in the new village of Martlesham Heath in 1979.

more than the date of a refurbishment which had given it a new facade.

In Cambridge an old pub reopened with a new name. The George in Thompsons Lane had been leased by the brewers from St John's College in 1888 at a rental of £12.50 a year, and it closed after the lease expired in 1968. It was reopened in 1976 as the Spade and Becket, the latter being a tool used in the Fens for cutting turves of peat. There was some disappointment at the change of name, since it was pointed out that in the past it had been possible to start at the George, follow the river to the Fort St George on Midsummer Common, then continue to the Green Dragon in Chesterton, an interesting run of names.

New pubs built included the Douglas Bader in the new village of Martlesham Heath, built on the site of the airfield that had for many years been home to the RAF's Aeroplane and Armament Experimental Establishment, and also a Battle of Britain fighter station. Group Captain Sir Douglas Bader himself pulled the first pint when it opened in 1979, and then went outside to watch a flypast by a Spitfire and Hurricane of the Battle of Britain Memorial Flight.

The horseracing town of Newmarket was also expanding, and in 1975 Tolly Cobbold opened a new public house as part of the

The interior of the Douglas Bader. The accent on food is noticeable in this view.

"Four Suffolk Originals", an advertisement for Tolly's Original Bitter, launched in 1979.

Rookery shopping centre there. Eschewing the obvious "Horse and Groom" or any other racing allusion, those in charge chose to name it The Prohibition; customers stepping into the bar were greeted by a large portrait of Al Capone. Unusually, The Prohibition incorporated a cellar that was upstairs.

A personality from the world of entertainment, Terry Wogan, pulled the first pint at the new Newmarket pub. Norfolk farmer and

The racking room in Cliff Brewery. By the time this photograph was taken the old wooden barrels had given way to metal casks. EADT

Anglia Television personality Dick Joice did the honours when another new pub, the Four Leafed Clover, opened in Norwich.

And in 1981 the Ipswich brewery company bought its first London public house, the Westmoreland Arms in George Street, W.1, just off Baker Street.

Tolly Cobbold and CAMRA, the Campaign for Real Ale, had not always been on the best of terms, since the Camra enthusiasts were critical of anything that was considered to detract from the traditional, but in the late seventies Cliff Brewery began to put more emphasis on the production of real ale. Bacchante made her return to the company's beer mats, albeit minus the baby, as the brewery advertising stressed that Tolly Cobbold beer was "traditional", and more of the Tolly Cobbold houses were equipped with beer engines as an alternative to dispensing the beer by gas pressure. The company, however, always insisted that it was crucial that publicans and club barmen should look after cask conditioned beer with the greatest diligence.

Nevertheless, in 1979 the brewery launched a new bitter, Tolly Original, which was aimed at the real ale market; it was sold only in cask-conditioned form and was served either by handpump or by gravity. Based on traditional recipes used in earlier years, it reintroduced the technique of dry hopping, that is, adding hops to the beer after it had been racked into casks.

A curious result of the takeover of Tolly Cobbold by the Ellerman group was the naming by Mrs Eileen Laister, wife of Tolly

Gordon's
Special Dry
London Gin
40% VOL.
Gordon's

Cobbold chairman Peter Laister, of a new Ellerman Lines container ship launched in 1979 at Appledore in Devon. After breaking a bottle of champagne supplied by Barwell & Jones across the ship's bows, Mrs Laister named her City of Ipswich — though in truth Ipswich is a town and not a city.

At the time the Ellerman group acquired Cameron's brewery in Hartlepool a young man named Bob Wales was working his way up the Hartlepool ladder from office boy to chief accountant. He had joined the brewery straight from school at the age of seventeen. In 1982 he moved to Ipswich to fill the post of finance director at Tolly Cobbold; it was just another step up the career ladder on the way to something better as far as he could then see.

Fate decreed otherwise. At the beginning of 1983 the Ellerman group was getting into financial difficulties because of the decline in the world of shipping, and Tolly Cobbold along with other companies within the group was put up for sale. Plans for a management buyout at Ipswich came to naught when it was announced that the entire Ellerman group had been sold to the Barclay brothers, David and Frederick, who had made their money out of property development and hotels.

"I had only come down here for three years to get finance director's experience and then go on and do something else again," says Bob Wales. "But with the arrival of the Barclays it was such a fascinating time, during the period when the property boom was starting off, that I spent the next five or six years as close to them as possible and learning as much as I could. They were very astute; their lives were built around property, and they could see the opportunity in the assets that they had here and at Cameron's."

It was at this period that Brian Cowie, a Glaswegian who had joined Scottish and Newcastle Breweries on coming down from university, and had later been with Allied Breweries in the Midlands, came to Cliff Brewery as sales and marketing director. He and Bob Wales soon began to work as a team, and had already formed a good relationship by the time the Tolly Cobbold brewery changed hands yet again and became part of the Brent Walker leisure group headed by former boxer George Walker.

No sooner was the takeover completed than Brent Walker sold a number of Tolly Cobbold public houses to Grand Metropolitan. It was plain to both Bob and Brian that Brent Walker would not keep two breweries open, and it was equally clear that the choice for closure would fall on Cliff Brewery. Cameron's had benefited from massive investment because Hartlepool was in a Special Development Area, which was receiving all kinds of grants, while the Ipswich brewery had not.

Others, too, could see the way things were going, and in April, 1989, a national newspaper reported that Brent Walker development director Timothy Quinlan had revealed that closure plans were under examination. Cameron's brewery was more cost-effective and was capable of producing all the beer and lager

Opposite page: Bob Wales, who came to the Cliff Brewery in 1982 for three years — and stayed on.

Glaswegian Brian Cowie, who joined Tolly Cobbold during the time it was owned by the Barclay brothers.

needed by the group, while the sale of Cliff Brewery could produce a large sum of money to reduce Brent Walker borrowing. The item appeared on the same day that Brent Walker announced end of year results in which pre-tax profits had doubled to nearly £42 million.

A month later Patrick Cobbold and Lord Tollemache both resigned their directorships of Tolly Cobbold, leaving Richard Cobbold as the sole representative of the families.

Then, at the beginning of June, came the announcement that everyone concerned with brewing in Ipswich had dreaded. Production of Tolly beers was to be transferred to the Lion Brewery at Hartlepool, and Brent Walker's public house and retail operations were to be streamlined; sixty-six production workers would lose their jobs when Cliff Brewery ceased production on 14th July.

An end, and a new beginning 8

AS CLOSURE approached anger mounted in Suffolk over the decision to move production of Tolly Cobbold beers to another part of the country. CAMRA reacted furiously to the news, an action group was formed to campaign against the closure, Ipswich Borough Council chief executive James Hehir travelled to London to face George Walker himself, and a correspondent in the *Evening Star* protested at "further destruction of local identity and character".

Families of brewery employees, and the company's tenants and their families, were given a last invitation to visit the brewery and to partake of a last glass of real Tolly Cobbold beer, brewed in Ipswich. Members of the Suffolk Industrial Archaeology Society, anxious to inspect the brewery before it was closed and, they feared, demolished, were also invited to one of the final open evenings.

Those industrial archaeologists found themselves regarded as gate-crashers at a very sombre family gathering, but one of the brewery staff was willing to show them around. Thus they began a conducted tour of the brewery that might have served as a model for others to come. And over a glass of beer afterwards they discussed how to prevent the 1723 copper, the E.R. & F. Turner steam engine and brewery archives from being removed to Hartlepool, where it was rumoured they were to be displayed in a Brent Walker museum of brewing. "They are a part of our heritage, and we really wouldn't like to see them taken elsewhere," a society spokesman said later in a newspaper interview.

Lord Tollemache

Meanwhile Ipswich Borough Council, having failed to persuade George Walker to reconsider his decision to close the brewery, took steps to prevent demolition of the premises. After hearing the council's director of development services, Geoffrey Ramsdale, say that "the main brewery building has a strong architectural character — the building forms a prominent and distinctive landmark to this part of the River Orwell," the planning and development committee decided to list the main brewery building as a building of historic and architectural interest, grade II.

To counter the threatened removal of equipment from the brewery, the council, whose leader, Jamie Cann, took a leading part in moves to ensure the continuation of brewing in Ipswich, later extended the listing to include not only the ancient copper and the steam engine but all the brewery equipment.

What nobody knew at the time the brewery employees were producing eighty barrels of premium ale, named Final Brew, was that moves had already been made by Bob Wales and Brian Cowie to acquire and reopen the brewery. For Bob Wales it was a case of

The message was clear: this effigy appeared at the brewery as the closure day neared. EADT

lightning striking in the same place a second time, as he and Brian planned another attempt at a management buyout.

They produced a thirty-page business plan, setting out their philosophy as concisely as possible with the intention of convincing possible backers that they could succeed in making the project pay. Later Sir John Harvey-Jones, well known for his *Troubleshooter* programme on BBC television, was to say that their business plan gave him the fullest description of what they were aiming for that he had ever had from any company.

Initially they received a negative answer from George Walker, but as the property market fell from day to day and the financial pressure on Brent Walker built up they were encouraged to try again. "I remember that we extracted a promise from George that he would finally let us know before Christmas, 1989," says Brian Cowie.

"Christmas Day that year was a Monday, so when Friday, the 22nd of December, came and went and we hadn't heard anything and George was off on his holiday to Zermatt I remember saying to Bob, 'Well, that's it, you know, we're not going to hear anything till some time in the New Year'.

"However, George was nothing if not a man of his word, and if he had shaken hands on something he would honour it. On the Christmas Eve, a Sunday, about eight o'clock, Bob got a telephone call from Jim Mackenzie, the chairman and chief executive of Cameron's brewery, who was close to the Brent Walker organisation and to George, to say that George had agreed the deal and could we get down there mid-week to settle the details, and could he have the cash.

"When Bob rang to tell me this I thought he was just trying to pull my leg, I couldn't believe it. But it wasn't a wind-up.

"I think it was the Wednesday, the day after Boxing Day, we went down, and it was more or less 'let's agree the details and how quickly can you get the cash?' As if we had a few boxes of used fivers! And that's when the fun really started."

After all the Christmas haste, it took another six months before the deal was finalised. On 22nd June, 1990, the agreements were signed in a London solicitors' office, and on 14th July, exactly a year after brewing had ceased, company chairman the Hon. Peter Strutt, restored to his old position, raised the Tolly Cobbold flag over the brewery.

Members of the Cobbold and Tollemache families, including Patrick Cobbold and Lord Tollemache, along with licensees, local businessmen and senior brewery managers, took shares in the new company. But there was still a long way to go, and Brent Walker themselves put Bob and Brian in touch with Svenska Handelsbanken, who helped to provide the £4 million needed to set up the buyout and put the brewery back into production.

During the whole of that year, and until brewing could be started again at Ipswich, Tolly Cobbold beers were supplied from the Hartlepool brewery. This did not satisfy Brent Walker's Suffolk customers, however, and CAMRA refused to feature the "Suffolk" ales from the north-east at the Ipswich Beer Festival. It was the first

Opposite page: Members of the action group set up to oppose the closure hold a mock funeral at the Woolpack in Ipswich. The "corpse" is labelled "Brewing in Ipswich". EADT

BREWING
IN IPSWICH
1746 – 1989
"TILL YOU
RISE AGAIN

time in the history of the festival that the Tolly Cobbold brands had not been available.

There were, indeed, problems with the initial batches of "Tolly" from Hartlepool, and large quantities were sent back by Suffolk licensees because they said the beer was undrinkable. Even when the teething troubles were overcome local connoisseurs remained highly critical: "Friends and I have been sampling the new beer, unfortunately only the Bitter and Mild, as Original and Four X seem to be very thin on the ground . . . The Bitter is vastly different, being much more hoppier and drier in taste, and the Mild is darker, heavier, and with a more pronounced 'toffee' taste reminiscent of Northern brews. To say that these beers are 'the same as Tolly Cobbold' is patently ridiculous."

There was delight in "Tolly Country" — as East Anglia had been described in an earlier advertising campaign — at the raising of the flag, but beer did not begin to flow immediately. Workers had to be recruited — largely, though not entirely, from the old workforce — all the equipment in the brewery had to be stripped down and recommissioned, and then test brews had to be done to ensure that the brewery was producing high quality beers.

"It took us all of three months to do that, and it was on 24th September that we went into trade with the first of our new brews,"

The rebirth of a brewery: workers, re-employed by the new independent company, enjoy a celebratory drink as company chairman the Hon. Peter Strutt raises the Tolly Cobbold flag over the brewery on 14th July, 1990, a year to the day after brewing had ceased. EADT

says Bob Wales, who became joint managing director with Brian Cowie. "During that time we hadn't been earning a penny, but we'd been paying 17½ per cent interest on our funds."

"You only get one opportunity to launch beers, and of course we wanted to make sure not only that the brewery was up and running but that it was producing the right type of beer," adds Brian Cowie, who with completion of the deal had given up his position as Brent Walker's southern trade director. "We did in fact change some of the beers from what had been brewed previously.

"We did a lot of extensive research to make sure that the beers were not only satisfactory to us but satisfactory to our customers, and we had a lot of publicans from far and wide who came in to have tasting sessions. Among them were some from the most famous Tolly Cobbold pubs including Dick Mainwaring (Butt and Oyster, Pin Mill), Peter Lockwood (Woolpack, Ipswich), Mick Chaplin (Bristol Arms, Shotley), Bob Spence (The Swan, Holbrook), Mick

The rebirth of a brew: Patrick Cobbold was at the Woolpack in September, 1990, to help launch the new Tolly Cobbold brew, brought from the brewery on a dray drawn by two Suffolk Punches. With him are groom Tony Moore and the landlord of the Woolpack, Peter Lockwood. EADT

Lungley (The Angel, Woodbridge), and Chris Punchard (The Plough, Ipswich).

"We increased the gravity of some of the beers and made them all-malt brews, and just improved the quality and the way in which they were brewed. Unless you have a quality product and a quality organisation you won't succeeed, and so we determined to build in quality really from the outset."

The return of real Tolly Cobbold beers later in the year was greeted with delight by beer drinkers in the region. It was a much leaner company that was producing them, but during those first few years the beers won a number of awards at CAMRA festivals; in 1994 Tolly Mild was in the top six at the Great British Beer Festival.

As part of the deal done with Brent Walker the latter undertook to take beer from Cliff Brewery for a five-year period, and Tolly Cobbold also gained a contract to take over distribution to some 250 Brent Walker houses in the area. The collapse of the Brent Walker empire put these arrangements in jeopardy, but fortunately it proved possible to renegotiate the agreement with Pubmaster, the new company formed to operate the former Brent Walker pubs.

Company chairman the Hon. Peter Strutt and joint managing director Brian Cowie promoting the new brews at the sixth Suffolk Licensed Trade Fair at the Ipswich Moat House in August, 1991. EADT

A Cobbold advertisement from the 1930s bearing the image of the brewer sampling his own brew. Inset below is the up-dated version used on company notepaper and promotional material today.

COBBOLD & CO. LTD.,

Cliff Brewery,

IPSWICH.

The Family of Cobbold have been brewers for over TWO CENTURIES.

The Cliff Brewery in Ipswich was entirely rebuilt in 1894 and equipped with the most modern machinery. They are noted for—

DARK STOCK ALE
LIGHT PALE ALE
AND STOUT

which are brewed under the most hygienic conditions.

WINES AND SPIRITS.

30, Lower Brook Street,

IPSWICH.

Opposite page: Cardinal Wolsey was featured on the label of the 1995 Year Beer, and is here impersonated by Brian Cowie. EADT

Left: Major Angus Dubes with Bob Wales and label designer Gordon Smith at the naming of the 1993 Year Beer, Cantab. The label featured Bacchante, the old Tolly Cobbold trade mark.

Below: A bottle of Cobbold's IPA, the 1995 Year Beer, showing Cardinal Wolsey and the college gateway.

To celebrate the return of brewing to Ipswich it was decided to brew a special bottled beer, Ipswich Pride, which would be on sale throughout 1991. Appropriately, it was named by Lord Tollemache.

Ipswich Pride was the start of a new tradition. Each year since, a special Year Beer has been brewed, its name a closely guarded secret until the formal ceremony in the Copper Room of the brewery at which the new beer is launched. In 1992 it was Cobnut, named by Patrick Cobbold, in 1993 Cantab, named by Major Angus Dubes, and in 1994 Beano Stout, named by Peter Strutt. The following year it was Richard Cobbold's turn to name the Year Beer, Cobbold's IPA, and for 1996 Jamie Cann, now the town's Member of Parliament, was invited to name Cobbold's 250 Special, a celebratory brew for the 250th anniversary of brewing in Ipswich.

The labels designed for the Year Beers by Gordon Smith have won prizes in the Label of the Year competition, providing something of a bonus for the company as it struggled to make its way in the face of a continuing recession.

The joint managing directors had somewhat revolutionary ideas for the future of the brewery, which throughout all the changes and developments since it was built in 1896 had remained basically a Victorian brewery. Extensions there had been, but almost uniquely they had neither masked nor greatly affected the main brewery building; the geography of the site ensured that all the new development was to the east, leaving the magnificent Victorian brewery still a dominant feature of the riverside setting.

Both Bob and Brian had travelled to the United States, and had seen how the Americans displayed their heritage. They had also noticed how Scottish distilleries had for many years organised tours for visitors.

THE
BREWERY
TAP

Left: The designs by Baynes & Co. for the interior and exterior of the Brewery Tap, formerly Cliff House.

Right: The Brewery Tap in being, crowded with people drinking Tolly Cobbold beers.

Below: Work begins on the conversion in March, 1992. EADT

Left: Two of the entertainers at the Victorian party with which the Brewery Tap was opened on 24th June, 1992.

Below: East Suffolk Morris Men performing at the opening party, with the Brewery Tap and the brewery itself in the background.

"The thing that always struck us was that when you went into whichever distillery it was, you saw the production process, you saw the way the product was lovingly produced and cared for, and at the end of it all you bought the inevitable bottle of Scotch in the shop," explains Brian Cowie, his rich Scots voice displaying his enthusiasm. "And of course, once you had drunk it you were sold for life, you'd go out and you'd buy the stuff for ever.

"We thought, here we have this magnificent building, with all this magnificent equipment on display, and yet in the past it'd hardly been shown to anyone. It just seemed the obvious thing to do to show it to the public. It just seemed so obvious to bring people around, to show them how we care, it was going to be our form of marketing."

Thus was born the brewery tour. Since the first brewery tour took place on 16th September, 1992, more than 50,000 people have climbed the iron stairs to the top floor of the brewery and looked out over the port and town of Ipswich from that unusual vantage point.

Richard Cobbold, seen here with Bob Wales, launched the 1995 Year Beer, Cobbold's IPA. The painting is the artwork for the Year Beer label.

The 18th-century Cliff House, once home for members of the Cobbold family, was with great care converted into the Brewery Tap. Bob and Brian went to a top design firm, Baynes & Co., whose brief was to produce a traditional pub with an old-fashioned atmosphere and a "lived-in" look. They were both delighted with the result.

When it was officially opened on 24th June, 1992, with a colourful Victorian party, at which guests were entertained by fire eaters, jugglers and Morris dancers, the Brewery Tap became not just the newest "old" pub in Ipswich but the gateway to the brewery for those partaking of the brewery tour. A back door serves to take parties almost directly into the Victorian brewery.

Women's Institutes, senior citizens' clubs, and a host of other organisations have booked for the brewery tours, while thousands of individuals have dropped into the Brewery Tap to join the regular tours led by trained guides who are well prepared to answer questions about the brewing process which is going on all the time.

It was, and is, a wonderful marketing ploy for a small company that could not afford to spend money on television advertising like the "Tolly Country" campaign of the 1970s and on large-scale advertisements in the press.

"Yes, although we've fallen in love with this wonderful brewery, this history, this heritage, this tradition," says Brian Cowie, "a buyout teaches you that you have got to be absolutely practical, because you have to convince some hard headed, dare I say it, fairly cynical people that this will work."

Below: Bob Wales and Ipswich Buses commercial director Malcolm Robson drink to the success of the special bus service which brings visitors to the brewery tours. The open-top bus had been repainted in Ipswich Tramways colours to celebrate ninety years of municipal transport in the town. EADT

Troubleshooter 9

Sir John Harvey-Jones

SIR JOHN Harvey-Jones is probably Britain's best-known businessman. A former chairman of ICI, he became known to the man and woman in the street when he made the television series Troubleshooter, which first appeared on the screen in 1990.

Though he firmly denies being a business guru, he came to be seen as one who could put his finger on the weaknesses in other people's businesses. However, he believes that while he can point out what he would do in certain circumstances, it is up to those running the businesses to decide what to do and how it should be done. He recognises the horrendous problems facing people in business, particularly in raising money; and those problems were certainly faced by those seeking to re-establish the Tolly Cobbold brewery in the early 1990s.

In 1992 it was decided to produce a second series of *Troubleshooter*, and an immense variety of companies and organisations came forward in response to contacts with business bodies and advertisements in management magazines. A number were picked out to be the subject of the new series, but there was still something missing.

It was at that stage that television producer Judi Rose rang Tolly Cobbold asking if they were prepared to submit to Sir John's searching analysis.

"Well, we had seen the first series," says Brian Cowie. "Those were companies in difficulties. We thought, my goodness, do we really want to be on the *Troubleshooter* programme, we're not a company in difficulty. We are a company starting out, we've got some challenges, but we're not in difficulty."

However, the producer managed to convince the two joint managing directors that the series was not just about companies in trouble. She was looking for a subject for the last programme in the series, due to be broadcast around Christmas, 1992, and a brewery that had been the subject of a management buyout seemed to provide an appropriate and interesting subject.

"I have to say that there was a risk that Sir John would look at our company and say, 'Well, you know, brewing's a difficult business and you shouldn't be in it'," says Brian Cowie. "There was always that great risk."

"It was extremely brave, even totally foolhardy, to expose your business to that kind of inquisition," adds Bob Wales. "As it turned out — I didn't realise it at the time — we were the only company in the entire twelve programmes in the two series that was headhunted. All the other businesses had volunteered. It didn't take us too long to decide that this was an opportunity not to be missed."

Sir John Harvey-Jones meets Roger Protz, editor of *What's Brewing*, at the Butt and Oyster at Pin Mill, a famous riverside pub that was for many years a Cobbold house.

Sir John duly arrived at Cliff Brewery, after meeting the joint managing directors outside the Old Custom House beside Ipswich Dock. With a fine sense of history, Sir John later wrote that it was a splendidly symbolic meeting place; he was thinking of Thomas Cobbold shipping his spring water down the river of which the dock once formed a part.

Having heard from Bob and Brian of their dream of running a working brewery museum and keeping up the tradition of brewing in Ipswich, Sir John was shown around the brewery by Chris Gregson, the head brewer, who had joined the Tolly Cobbold team very soon after the buyout. He was clearly impressed by Chris, whom he described as small in stature but packing a big punch.

Indeed, he was impressed by the Tolly Cobbold team in its entirety. "The sixteen people who are employed in the brewery itself are the most tremendous bunch," he later said. "When they are not brewing they are painting and preparing the brewery for its future role as a working museum."

That was certainly the hallmark of the new team, which included many of the former employees who had been made redundant when Brent Walker closed the brewery; they were all prepared to do anything that was needed to make a success of the brewery.

The same flexibility was apparent to Sir John when he studied

Sir John, pint in hand, enjoys a chat with Dick Mainwaring, licensee of the Butt and Oyster, who was able to tell him just why Suffolk people were anxious to retain their own brewery at Ipswich.

the distribution side of the business with John Artiss, who started his life as a drayman and was, as Sir John put it, "living proof of the fact that experience can make up for any amount of theory". Noting that John Artiss and his fellow managers all went out on delivery rounds themselves, Sir John was delighted to find that the Transport and General Workers' Union allowed such flexibility and supported the efforts that were being made to ensure a really good service to customers — "a far cry from the popular picture of how unions work," he observed.

In the course of making the programme, which went out on 22nd December, 1992, Sir John had lunch with Roger Protz, editor of *What's Brewing*, and a CAMRA spokesman, and also went to Burton-on-Trent to consult Don Marshall, a senior director of Allied Breweries.

And then came the day when Sir John, on board a sailing barge on the Orwell, with a bitter wind blowing in from the sea, told Bob and Brian of his findings. He gave them rather better than a fifty per cent chance of success, very high odds indeed for a management buyout — in 1989 there had been a 14.7 per cent failure rate among firms which had been subject to a buyout.

He expressed misgivings about the museum project; in Burton-on-Trent he had been told that such a project was regarded merely as a loss leader in order to sell Allied Breweries products. What they should be concentrating on, he told them, was ensuring that they achieved the highest production of which the brewery was capable, and with that in mind they should try to extend their contract brewing.

The distribution element was, he said, the strongest part of the business, and he advised that careful attention should be given to

Tolly Cobbold distribution manager John Artiss impressed Sir John, who said that he was "living proof of the fact that experience can make up for any amount of theory".

that. If all else failed, he thought, the distribution side of the business might pull it through.

And he advised Bob and Brian not to spend any of their capital on acquiring public houses. They did need flagship outlets in East Anglia, but he was convinced that they could not afford to invest in buying pubs, though he thought they might take opportunities of leasing a number of houses.

He wrote later that Bob and Brian seemed to accept many of the points he made, and said they would go away and think about them. The last thing he told them was that they needed a slogan, for both the brewery tours and for the beers themselves.

But Sir John did not have everything his own way, for the joint managing directors were determined not to let him do all the work. However, they did take up his suggestion of a slogan to play a little trick on him.

"We wanted to create one or two unusual talking points for the TV programme, so along the way we did spring various surprises on Sir John," Brian remembers. "One of them was a spoof of a new beer called Troubleshooter.

"Sir John was absolutely thrilled to see his face on it, and this lovely wee phrase, 'It's the beer that does the business'.

"When it went out on television we were inundated with people

The spoof: Sir John is invited to draw a pint of "Troubleshooter", a surprise sprung on him by Bob Wales and Brian Cowie that delighted him.

asking us where they could get this beer. But of course at that time the beer had not been produced, it was just a spoof beer, just a pump clip, so we had to set up a research programme to develop this beer called Troubleshooter."

It did not prove possible to obtain permission from the BBC to call the new beer Troubleshooter, so instead it was named Tollyshooter. Sir John enthusiastically consented to having his portrait on the pump clip, so long as it was made clear that he was receiving no payment or royalties.

On 26th April, 1993, Sir John flew to Ipswich Airport and went on to the brewery to pull the first pint of Tollyshooter bitter. It was all excellent publicity for the brewery, and perhaps something rather more.

Sir John had recommended that Tolly Cobbold should introduce its beers to London, but there were fears that this would prove difficult and costly to achieve. After he had pulled the first pint of Tollyshooter, however, it was announced that the new bitter was to be sold in Nicholson's houses in the capital as a guest beer.

The real thing: Accompanied by head brewer Chris Gregson and company chairman the Hon. Peter Strutt, Sir John tries a glass of Tollyshooter bitter. He and Chris both wear their Tollyshooter ties.

Beer, ale and brewing 10

TECHNIQUES for producing alcoholic drinks from malted grain have been known for thousands of years. The ancient Egyptians had their own method of making such drinks by first baking a malt loaf and then infusing the bread to produce the alcoholic beverage. Head brewer Chris Gregson has copies of Egyptian hieroglyphs sent him by the British Museum which show this indirect brewing process.

In a later period a thick white drink made of millet, and fermented, was popular in the Middle East; it was known by the Turkish word "boza". Could that possibly be the origin of the English word "booze"? Robert Southey, who is perhaps best known for *The Life of Nelson*, remarked in one of his books that during campaigns in the Middle East "The Booza makers are a very necessary corporation in a camp"; most likely it was British soldiers taking part in those campaigns who brought the word home.

Medieval wills bear witness to the fact that Suffolk households brewed their own beer; household accounts from the Middle Ages, too, tell of the quantities of beer supplied to guests and to workers carrying out their customary services for the lord of the manor.

In 1615 Henry Piper, an Ipswich poldavisweaver, had an inventory made of his property, and in the brewhouse his appraisers found "a lyttle brasse panne and a leade" worth eleven shillings, eighteen "tubbes and keelers" and, perhaps thrown in a corner, "a beame and scales, a hennes Coope, an old hatchett and other old lumber". Others took their brewing more seriously: in 1637 Edward Bourne of Bury St Edmunds, gentleman, left "To my son Edward the following . . . in the brewhouse the brass and all the brewing vessels as they now stand".

Even in much more recent times farmers produced their own ale and beer for consumption on the farm; the best, no doubt, they kept for themselves, the less good went to the many workers employed in the fields. George Ewart Evans describes this domestic brewing in some detail in his book *Ask the Fellows who cut the Hay*, where he records the memories of the people of Blaxhall; it is a coincidence that the Ship at Blaxhall was one of the last places in Suffolk where one could find traditional singing and step-dancing.

There were usually two brewings every year, one just before harvest and another in time for Christmas. These were important occasions for the household, for much depended on the success of the operation, which took the whole of one day and the following night. It was the housewife's job to undertake the brewing, but she might call on other members of the family for help; in August, 1871, the logbook of Blaxhall school records "Great many absentees; required at home for brewing".

No head brewer in a large brewery has ever been more concerned over the success of a brewing; happy the housewife who found a mushroom of yeast forming and could say "Everything's all right now; the beer is a-smiling".

Many an alehouse and inn had its own brewhouse, a few of them continuing to make their own brews into the present century. Sometimes, perhaps, one such brewhouse supplied more than the one premises, for in 1636 Thomas Hudson of Woolpit, beer brewer, left to his elder son Thomas "my house in Woolpit commonly called the Maids Head, my house in which I dwell called the Crown, the brewing house and brewing vessels . . . on condition he pays my debts, the charges of my burial and my legacies".

The quality of the ale and beer produced in these brewhouses, and by many of the common brewers whose drinks were distributed to hostelries within a short distance of the brewery, was open to question. There were probably few who could, like John R. Dawson at Washbrook in 1864, guarantee that his ales were "the pure Extract of Malt and Hops".

Indeed, Sir Cuthbert Quilter of Bawdsey Manor actually acquired the Coach and Horses Brewery at Melton towards the end of the 19th century with the avowed intention of providing "pure beer" that was free of the adulterants then much in fashion among

Home brewing under way, seen in an early 19th century print. At a period when water might well be unfit to drink the brewing process sterilised the liquor and produced a beverage that was universally enjoyed.

A malting on Wherry Quay, Ipswich, that was at one time owned by the Cobbold family. The kiln can be seen rising above the roof of what has now become a public house called the Malt Kiln.

the country's brewers. Had he lived a hundred years later he would surely have been a patron of The Campaign for Real Ale.

Real beer is made with the four standard ingredients, malt, hops, yeast and water — never referred to as such by the brewer, who calls it liquor. Tommy Handley's Colonel Chinstrap would have approved.

Those are the ingredients used at the Cliff Brewery today. "Our brews are 100 per cent malt and we do not use any other sources of starch," says Chris Gregson with some pride. "All the colour in our beers is brewed in using coloured malts, and no additions of caramel or colouring are made."

In times gone by the Cobbolds had a number of maltings at the Cliff and in the town of Ipswich; Thomas Cobbold was a maltster before opening his brewery in Harwich in 1723. Today all the malt is bought in from "sales maltsters", with whom contracts are negotiated annually.

Malting is a very old-established trade in East Anglia. Ipswich was already a centre of the trade when in 1508 the town authorities moved against "aliens" — people who were not freemen of the borough — engaged in malting: "Forasmuch as the maintainance of this Towne is much in malt, and that many Forainers aliens within the same Town abiding, doe much hinder the Free Burgesses by theire Malting. Therefore it is ordered that noe Forrainer alien shall

A maltster ploughing a piece in a floor malting. It was necessary to plough the green malt both in order to aerate it and to prevent the rootlets from matting as the grain germinated.

by himselfe or any other, Malt any Barley, otes, or other graine, under the penalty of 6s. 8d. for every quarter soe Malted".

The process of malting consists basically of three stages: the steeping, in which the grain is immersed in water for a period which can be as long as several days; the germination, which in the old floor maltings took place with the barley spread on the malting floor; and the kilning, when the green malt is heated and dried over a smokeless fire to bring growth to an end. Whatever mechanical means may be employed to facilitate the making of malt, the process remains basically the same.

During germination natural enzymes in the corn begin to break down the protein and starch reserves in the grain, rendering them soluble. The maltster's skill is in judging just the right moment to transfer the green malt to the kiln and to bring the germination to an end.

"Kilning performs two functions," explains Chris Gregson. "The first is a drying process with relatively low temperatures and high air flows. The second is a curing process to give the malt additional flavour and colour, with air flows reduced and temperatures higher."

The basic process is varied to produce different types of malt. Lager malt is low in colour and flavour, so requires to be only lightly

The malt mill at the Cliff Brewery in which the carefully selected malts were ground for the next day's brew.

cured; pale ale malt, the major ingredient used at the Cliff Brewery, requires higher temperatures and lower air flows, while the chocolate malt used in Mild and Old Strong is produced at high temperatures not in a kiln but in special roasting drums.

"We think most of the roast house operators must have ulcers," says Chris Gregson with a grin, "because the balance between getting the correct colour and the whole lot catching fire is a very fine one!"

Pale ale malt is nowadays delivered to the brewery in 20-tonne bulk loads, but the coloured malts still come in sacks, just as they did in Victorian times when men had to carry the 150lb. sacks up several flights of stairs to the top of the brewery. Hoists and elevators have cut out such legwork, and today one operator can control the whole process of selecting, weighing and milling the malt from an automated control panel.

"On the day before each brew the brewhouse operator is given details of the grist required for the next day's brew," says Chris. "From the control panel we can select the type of malt required: the pale ale malt passes through a batch weigher so that we can control the amount of malt in each brew; coloured malts are weighed out carefully and added after the weigher.

"All the malt passes through a screen to remove any unwanted materials such as stones, metal, string and so on, and then it is put through the mill.

"The mill has two sets of rollers, top and bottom, and the width between the rollers can be accurately controlled. As with many things in the brewing process, there are certain compromises.

"If we don't grind the malt finely enough we don't get very good extracts — and so the Chief Accountant gives the Head Brewer a hard time! If we mill too finely the whole process can become clogged, leading to very long process times.

"At worst the brew can become totally wrecked by over milling, as the mash can set like wallpaper glue — who needs four tons of wallpaper glue!

"Ideally, milling should leave the husks more or less intact, to help filtration in the mash tun, but the starchy middle should be well exposed. Our laboratory regularly takes samples of the ground malt and analyses them for three fractions, Course, Grits and Flour."

From the mill the ground malt is transferred to the grist cases on the floor below, ready for the next day's brews.

The bitter flavour of beer and its spicy aroma is given by the hops, today grown in Kent, Herefordshire and Worcestershire. In days gone by they were also grown in Suffolk, largely in the Stowmarket area; of nearly two hundred acres of hops grown in Suffolk in 1839 three-quarters were to be found in Stowmarket, Creeting, Haughley, Dagworth, Old Newton, Onehouse, Combs and Great Finborough. At that time hops were subject to duty, and between 1829 and 1835 those parishes grew some 64,000lb. of hops every year and paid an average duty of well over £500.

On the Continent, from which hops were introduced to Britain in the early 17th century, hops are not fertilised and so have no seeds; in this country male hops growing in the hedgerows fertilise the cultivated female plants, which therefore produce seeds.

The hop picking in Kent was once the traditional holiday occupation of East Enders from London, but in recent years the operation has become mechanised and the labour force has been much diminished. After drying in an oast house, as it is called in

Kent, or a kiln, so called in Hereford and Worcester, the hop cones are rammed into tall sacks known as pockets; each pocket weighs about 150lb.

Two varieties of hops are used in beers brewed at the Cliff Brewery, Goldings and Challenger. They come to the brewery in the form of pellets, produced quite simply by grinding up the hops and pressing the ground hops into pellets. In this form they can be vacuum packed and stored without deterioration and wastage.

"Hops are apparently in the same family as cannabis," says Chris with a broad smile. "We had a student working in the brewery who tried roll-ups made with hop pellets, but they didn't appear to do a lot for him. We believe that most of the hallucinations you get from beer drinking come from the alcohol rather than the hop resins."

At 7 am on brewing days an operator "mashes in", mixing the ground malt or grist with hot liquor in the masher, which contains a number of paddles operated by an electric motor. The mash is then run into the mash tun, in which it stands for half an hour. The floor of this vessel is a false one with hundreds of tiny slits, each about thirty thousandths of an inch wide, cut in it. This false floor acts with the husks in the grist as a filter, allowing the liquid to pass through to run-off pipes below.

During the time the mash is in the mash tun the enzymes produced during malting are activated to break down the starch in

Bob Wales and Chris Gregson with a basket of hops ready to be added to the old copper.

The mash tun, in which the starch in the ground malt or grist was broken down into sugars.

the malt corn into sugars. In order to get the best extract of sugars from the mash the texture of the mash must be carefully maintained and the mineral content of the water must be correct; hard liquor is ideal for brewing thirst-quenching ales. It is also essential that the temperature is very carefully controlled — to within one degree Fahrenheit.

"After an hour most of the starch will be broken into sugars," says Chris. "We can collect the sugars by spraying hot liquor on to the top of the mash, a process known as sparging. The sparge liquor leaches down through the mash bed, dissolving the sugars that have been formed from the starch.

"The sweet sugary brown liquid so formed is called wort, a word that is of Anglo-Saxon origin. The wort runs out through the slits in the false floor and is collected before being sent on to the next stage in the process. The malt husks left in the mash tun and the slits in the false floor form an effective filter bed to ensure that the wort is clear.

"We continue sparging the mash until all the goodness has been removed from the malt. As we are a cask beer brewery and so don't filter our beers, we have to be very careful not to be too greedy and squeeze the last drop of extract out of the mash. The last running can contain materials that would lead to hazes in our beers."

Sparging normally takes two or three hours, and when the wort is drained off mechanical arms automatically discharge the spent grains into a silo. Before the advent of automatic discharge men had to get into the mash tun and shovel the grains out by hand, a very hot job as the grains were at about 160 degrees Fahrenheit. The men would wear many pairs of woollen socks to prevent their feet being scalded through their boots.

The spent grains are sold to a cattle feed merchant. In the old days farmers used to send their own waggons along to the breweries to load "brewers' grains" to feed to their animals.

As the mash tun is cleaned out before the next brew the wort collected from the tun is pumped on to one of the two coppers, where it is boiled. Hops are added at this stage, and as the wort is boiled the bitter substances in the hops are absorbed into the wort.

"Boiling not only makes the wort bitter, it also sterilises the wort, and from this stage on we are very careful to control the microbiology of the wort," explains Chris, who began his working life as a brewing scientist. "Boiling also removes proteins that have come from the malt. If these were left in the wort we could potentially get cloudy beers."

The proteins might have gone, but at this stage the wort contains debris from the hop pellets and from the proteins, and if it is not removed it will clog up the yeast during the fermentation. This debris is removed in a whirlpool separator; the inlet pipe on the whirlpool is angled in such a way that as the wort comes down from the copper it spins around in the separator, depositing the sediments in a cone in the middle of the tank. A nice clear hot bitter wort can be taken from the edge of the vessel.

"When brewing Bitter and Original we add some extra Golding aroma hops to the whirlpool to give our beers extra hop aroma," Chris tells visitors. "Because the aroma oils are volatile much of the oil is lost from the hops added during the copper boil, and by this late hopping we put the oils back into the wort."

The next process is fermentation, but before yeast can be added the wort has to be cooled in a heat exchanger; yeast is a living organism and would be killed by the heat. The old fermenting room of the Cliff Brewery is a fine example of Victorian civil engineering and of the architecture of William Bradford.

Because of a belief that direct sunlight was bad for the beer blue glass was used for the skylights and shutters were installed on the south-facing side. Today open fermenting vessels are no longer used, but the beers are still put into brown or green bottles to prevent them developing a sun-struck flavour, Chris points out.

When the wort is in the fermenting vessel a small amount of extra liquor is added to adjust the specific gravity of the wort to the correct level for the type of beer being produced. The specific gravity is really a measure of the quantities of sugar in the beer and is measured using a saccharometer, which takes its name from saccharose, pure crystalline sugar.

An original boiling copper from the Harwich brewery of 1723, used as a sugar dissolving vessel at the Cliff Brewery.

F V
Nº3

"We usually collect wort at 65 degrees Fahrenheit," says Chris. "As the fermentation begins, the temperature rises, but it's controlled using cooling water jackets. The temperature is held to about 70 degrees F. If the fermentation temperature is too high, all sorts of funny flavours start to develop — as often happens with home brewing.

"After nearly three days the yeast has fermented most of the sugars to produce alcohol and carbon dioxide gas. At this stage the yeast head is skimmed off using a suction pipe. The beer is then cooled gently to about 50 degrees F., and the beer is left to condition or mature for a few more days.

"There's a saying in the industry that brewers shouldn't make ungodly beers that haven't seen a Sabbath," Chris remarks. "All our beers therefore spend a minimum of seven days in vessel."

The yeast usually multiplies two-fold during fermentation, so there is always some to be stored and some to be disposed of. After being skimmed from the top of the beer it is sucked into a tank and then blown into a filter press which squeezes out any excess beer, which can be returned to the fermenter.

Just one thing remains to be done when fermentation is complete. It is put into casks.

Historically wooden casks made by the cooper were used, but in most breweries these have been replaced by metal casks which are

Opposite page: Stan Clarke tests the wort in the fermenting vessel. He will use a saccharometer to check how far the process of changing sugar into alcohol has proceeded.

The horizontal steam engine that was used to pump water from the adjacent well up to the top of the building and also to work all the brewery's machinery was built by the Ipswich firm of E.R. & F. Turner, well known as milling engineers.

easier to clean and generally more hygienic as well as longer lasting. Wooden casks came in different sizes: a hogshead held fifty-four gallons, a barrel thirty-six and a kil — short for kilderkin — eighteen; a firkin held nine gallons and a pin just half that amount.

An important man in a brewery such as the Cliff Brewery is the "sniffer" who inspects the casks after they have been through the "Goliath" washing machine, which not only washes them inside and out but also sterilises them with steam. As well as looking inside the cask, he can smell if there is anything wrong. Any odd smells or taints, and he rejects the cask.

The "sniffer" also removes any pieces of wooden bungs or shives that have been knocked into the cask, before putting a fresh keystone into the hole at the end of the cask, which then goes to the racking or filling heads. Having been filled to the brim, the cask is sealed with a wooden plug known as a shive.

As the beer flows into the cask a metered quantity of isinglass finings is added. These finings, made from the swim bladders of tropical seafish, are essential to ensure that the beer clears properly during storage.

"We are unusual as a brewery in that we make our own finings from shredded swim bladders," Chris claims. "If you looked at isinglass under a very powerful microscope you would see a series of very long threads or filaments. These filaments have the opposite magnetic charge to yeast and attract the yeast strongly. This forms in

The cooperage at the Cliff Brewery, with many of the coopers' tools laid out. Beer barrels were usually made of oak imported from the Baltic countries.

microscopic terms a large lump that sediments through the beer more quickly than yeast alone would."

The filled casks are stacked temporarily after racking, and then are taken to the temperature-controlled cellar in the brewery. Once it would have been jottings on a piece of paper, today it is a computer printout that tells staff how many casks of each type of beer are needed to be loaded for the next day's deliveries.

When Sir John Harvey-Jones made the *Troubleshooter* programme at Cliff Brewery in 1992 he stressed the need for investment, and was concerned about whether the provision for new investment in the new company's forward plans would be enough to allow them to compete in a very tough world. This advice was not forgotten, and in 1995 Tolly Cobbold installed a new and entirely up-to-date brewhouse within the old Victorian brewery.

Sir John pointed out that in the old brewery they were still totally dependent on the dedication of the operators and in particular of the head brewer and of the foreman to maintain the quality they sought. For absolute consistency, he said, they needed some micro computers to test and analyse the brews automatically. This kind of automatic control is available with the new plant, which represents the very latest in brewing technology.

Thomas Cobbold would doubtless have been delighted with such a degree of quality control when he moved his brewery from Harwich to Ipswich 250 years ago.

The old copper room, with the original copper from the Harwich brewery prominent on the right.

Tolly Cobbold people 11

IN TELLING the story of 250 years of brewing in Ipswich it has been impossible to mention all the many thousands of men and women who have played their varied parts in the tale. There has been no space to tell of men like Alfred Porter, who was associated with the firm for sixty-three years under four generations of the Cobbold family and died in 1896; of Robert King, who retired in 1899 after being associated with the brewery for fifty-three years; or of Pamela Cobbold, John Dupuis Cobbold's younger daughter, who during the First World War volunteered for work at Ransomes Sims & Jefferies and drove one of their lorries. They, and many more whose names are quite unknown, all played their part in making the brewery business what it was.

"This has always been a very happy old place, it was like coming from home to home." That was how Stan Clarke described the Cliff Brewery; and he should know, for he spent thirty-five years at the brewery after the amalgamation of the two family firms, making a total of fifty years. He was the first to rejoin the brewery after the buyout, as Brewery Supervisor; he retired in 1995

He had started at the brewery in the days of Cobbold & Company, but "I got the sack for messing about, I was full of life". He was also, no doubt, full of confidence, for having lost his job with Cobbolds he went to work at the Tollemache brewery in Upper Brook Street, and apart from National Service remained there until the move to the Cliff Brewery.

Stan has memories of some of the characters who worked there when he was a youngster. "There was an old man, Frank Wilding, there many years," he recalls. "He used to say 'Remember that, boy, take it under your hat, it will come in handy'."

Another stalwart of the Tollemache brewery was George Pelling, who retired at the age of sixty-eight in 1939 and enjoyed thirty-eight years of retirement. Born at Ditchling in Sussex, Mr Pelling had come to Suffolk in 1921 to be manager of the bottling department.

Mr Pelling received the customary congratulatory telegram from the Queen when he reached his hundredth birthday in 1971, and received another five years later on his 105th birthday. He also had a birthday card each year from the brewery.

It was no surprise to those who knew him well that he reached such an advanced age: his grandmother had reached ninety-nine, his mother ninety-seven and his brother ninety-eight, while his eldest nephew, living in the United States, celebrated his diamond wedding at the age of eighty-nine. He died in 1977, four months after reaching the age of 106.

Stan remembers, too, some of the characters of his later years at

Opposite page: Stan Clarke, who retired as brewery supervisor in 1995, worked in both the Cliff Brewery and the Tollemache brewery in Upper Brook Street. EADT

Owen Betts compares the price of a glass of beer in 1996 with the prices given on a Tollemache advertisement from the early years of the century. EADT

the Cliff Brewery. People like Owen Betts, "he could turn anything into a joke".

For Stan work in the fermenting room, or the brewing room as it was generally known to the brewery workers, became a way of life rather than a mere job. "You can't mess beer about, beer has to be nursed," he says. "People used to laugh at me when I used to come back here at night. All the brewers used to come in at night, to see that the fermentations were goin' on all right. Weekends, Saturdays and Sundays, they all had to be looked after.

"Check temperatures and gravities, and check that it was on course for what you wanted. You didn't want the temperature to get too high. And you had to make sure there was no leaks in the hoses or anything. At that time you used to come in to see the blokes that was coming in for the night.

"This was a happy old place, our head brewer was very strict but always fair. If a man was in any trouble at home they'd always help him out. They **were** like a family.

"As for John and Patrick, they used to walk round the brewery and call out 'Are you all right, Stan?' They knew most people by name. We always used to call them Mr John and Mr Patrick, it was as simple as that."

Mr John was something of a character. He had gone into the

Army in 1944 straight from Eton and served for three years, so it was only in 1947 that he joined Cobbold & Company as general manager, later becoming managing director.

Being a nephew of Harold Macmillan, it seemed likely that John Cobbold would make a career in politics, but that was not to be. He fought the Ipswich constituency three times for the Conservatives between 1955 and 1959, but lost all three elections. Disillusioned with politics, he declared in 1972 that he would devote his time to the brewery and Ipswich Town Football Club, of which he had become chairman in 1957.

Perhaps the most apt comment at the time of his death in 1983 came from a man who might have been his opponent had he remained in politics, Ken Weetch, Labour MP for Ipswich from 1974 to 1987. "He was a Suffolk man through and through," said Ken, "and believed in the distinctive contribution that East Anglia and this part of it in particular could make to national life."

John's brother Patrick took over the chairmanship of Ipswich Town Football Club in 1976, two years before the club astounded national newspaper sports writers by winning the FA Cup. His comments on reports written at the time of the club's successful trip to Wembley by journalists who appear to have penetrated only as far as the Sporting Farmer adjacent to the Ipswich cattle market have not been recorded, but they would certainly have been worth hearing; his dry sense of humour was widely known.

He resigned as chairman of the football club in 1991, and later

Mr John.

Carl Giles's view of a Parliamentary by-election in October, 1957 in which John Cobbold was the unsuccessful Conservative candidate. His Liberal opponent on this occasion was Miss Manuela Sykes, and it was "the others'" candidate, Dingle Foot, who captured the seat.

"All the others want now is an Old Etonian brewer who can play like Stan Matthews, cook like Philip Harben, stand on his head and sing like Elvis Presley."

Left: One of the lorries from the Cliff Brewery ready to take part in a war savings procession in Ipswich, 1919.

Below: Tenants and employees gathered at Holywells in 1919 for the festivities that accompanied the wedding of John Murray Cobbold and Lady Blanche Cavendish. Prominent in the middle of the front row is Jos. Lewis, who retired in 1922 after 47 years at the brewery.

became president in succession to his mother, Lady Blanche.

Patrick took shares in the new company after the management buyout in 1990 and gave his full support to the joint managing directors in their efforts to retain brewing in Ipswich. His death in 1994 at the age of sixty was a severe blow.

The Hon. Peter Strutt, the present chairman of Tollemache and Cobbold Brewery Ltd., is a grandson of Douglas Tollemache, one of the founders of the Tollemache business. He joined the family brewery in 1947 after three years with the Coldstream Guards, who had fought their way through north-west Europe after the invasion of 1944. He underwent a one-year brewing course, and then began learning the job at the Tolly brewery, even becoming skilled at rolling barrels of beer across the yard.

The Hon. Peter Strutt, a grandson of one of the founders of Tollemache's Breweries Ltd.

He and John Cobbold were personal friends, even if business rivals, so there was no great difficulty for him when the two family companies were amalgamated in 1957. As managing director of Tollemache & Cobbold Breweries Ltd. he steered the brewery through some very stormy waters. Happily, the brewery survived, and on the first anniversary of its closure Peter Strutt raised the flag of the new company on the rooftop flagpole.

The directors and the workers in the brewery were only a small part of the Tolly Cobbold organisation, for there were also the men and women who kept the Tolly Cobbold pubs; they, too, were considered part of the family. When the company was bought out in 1990 some of the leading landlords of former Tolly Cobbold houses were given the opportunity of becoming shareholders in the new company.

Some landlords and landladies had plenty of time to stamp their personality on the houses in which they served. Miss Winnie Nunn had lived at the Castle Inn, Bredfield, for seventy-six years when she retired in 1975 after thirty-three years as licensee. She was then eighty. When asked to name the biggest change in the years she had lived at the Castle Inn, it was not any alteration in the beer or the rise in pub catering but the price that came to her mind. In her younger days, she pointed out, a pint of beer had been just two old pennies — less than a penny of the new coinage that had been introduced in 1970.

Given such longevity, it is perhaps not surprising that when Tolly Cobbold announced in 1975 that it was introducing compulsory retirement at the age of sixty-five there was an outcry from among the tenants. Some were way beyond the new retiring age, like Fred Boggis and his wife Ethel at the Admiral's Head, Little Bealings, and the company allowed them to remain as long as they wished. Fred and Ethel had been tenants of the Admiral's Head for fifty-six years when in 1980 they decided to call it a day; "You can't go on for ever," said Fred as he drew his last pint from the cask.

Some of the landlords seemed to be almost as old as their inns. When the bicentenary was being celebrated in 1923 Henry Heffer, of the George and Dragon at Farnham, on what had been called the Little Yarmouth Turnpike and is now the A12, was hailed as the

George Keeble beside his Thornycroft lorry, with a full load of crates of bottled beers.

longest-serving of Cobbold's tenants; he had been there since 1878 and also carried on the trade of blacksmith, wheelwright and agricultural implement maker in the adjoining premises. Within a year or so he had been succeeded by another generation, Herbert Heffer, who remained at the George and Dragon for more than a year or two.

R.A. Whitehead in his delightful book *The Beloved Coast* tells a story of "Harbut", who as a long-standing customer of the Leiston engineering works of Richard Garrett was never denied credit by that company. It was well known that he would pay whenever he chanced by the works. However, Garrett's was taken over in 1932 by the Manchester firm of Beyer Peacock & Co. Ltd., who installed a Mancunian accountant as general manager. During one of his visits to the Leiston works "Harbut" was being attended to by Cyril Thurston, in charge of the stores and spare parts department, when the new general manager, Arthur Bambrough, came striding down the yard.

Prompted either by a sense of duty or by a sense of mischief, Thurston introduced the two men. "Am I right in supposing that you are the same Mr Heffer who has owed the company a sum of money for many months past?" inquired the general manager, with a distinct lack of cordiality. It was a trivial sum, and "Harbut", a man who was absolutely indifferent to outward appearances and to what people thought of him, was not inclined to take the rebuff too seriously.

"That's quite right, Mr Bambrough," agreed Heffer, "wholly sorry I am but I expect to sell a machine or two shortly and then I'll be able to pay."

Reaching out, he took the hem of Bambrough's neat black jacket between his fingers. "That's a very nice jacket you've got on, Mr Bambrough, and, as you can see, mine's not up to much. Do you happen to have an old jacket at home you could spare I'd be wholly grateful for it, or an old raincoat either, for mine's past its best."

The general manager turned on his heel with an audible snort and stalked off. "Whoi," said Heffer to Cyril with a grin, "he don't seem to hev no sense o' hoomer."

The Heffers were not alone in having a long association with a particular house. One family was linked with the Ship Inn at Blaxhall for more than a hundred years from 1878, when Samuel Meadows took over. In 1884 Samuel passed the pub to his son-in-law, John Hewitt, who remained at the helm for forty-three years. Then in 1927 John Hewitt's son Arthur took over at the age of twenty-seven; he was at that time Cobbolds' youngest publican.

Illness forced Arthur and his wife Muriel to give up the Ship after thirty-eight years, and they then passed the licence to Arthur's niece Marguerite Saunders and her husband Horace, who gave up farming at Leiston to take over the Ship, one of the last places in Suffolk where traditional singing and step-dancing could be experienced. The couple were better known to their customers as "Midge" and "Jack". The family link was broken only in 1979, when Jack and Midge decided they wanted more time to themselves.

* * *

A few landlords had a lifetime association with a particular pub. One such was Tom Jeffrey, who retired from the Barham Sorrel Horse in 1977 after a quarter of a century as licensee. He might have taken the licence only in 1952, but his connection with the Sorrel Horse went back to 1919 when at the age of eight he moved in to live with his uncle and aunt; his uncle had become landlord six years earlier.

Tom was born at Wood Farm, Stonham Aspal. His mother's sister and her husband had the neighbouring Green Farm, and it was from there that they moved to take over the Sorrel Horse, which then belonged to the Shrubland estate. It was no great change, for the Sorrel Horse was in those days a farm as well as a public house, with 127 acres.

Indeed, the Sorrel Horse had at one time been a farmhouse, the original pub having stood further along the Ipswich-Norwich road. When the new landlord and landlady moved in, the road was surfaced only with flints bound in chalk, and the passing trade was largely waggoners and farm horsemen who stopped by for refreshment while on their way to Ipswich with loads of corn or other farm produce for market.

I remember calling in at the Sorrel Horse one day in 1977 to talk to Tom Jeffrey, who had been recommended to me as "a bit of a character". It was a little bit like stepping back into the past, closing the door of the Sorrel Horse behind you.

Tom told me the story of the occasion when one of the first motor-cars passed by on its way from Ipswich to Norwich. The

Opposite page: Chris Punchard, landlord of the Turk's Head at Hasketon, is an avid collector of Cobbold memorabilia. On the wall behind him is a portrait of John Chevallier Cobbold. EADT

engines of those early cars were prone to overheating, and to a good many other troubles besides, and it so happened that the driver of this one stopped at the Sorrel Horse to ask for some water to fill up the radiator.

Tom's uncle, who by all accounts was as much a character as Tom himself, fetched a jug of water and the radiator was topped up, whereupon the driver climbed back into his seat and prepared to resume his interrupted journey. He was doubtless in a hurry, as most motorists are, and did not like to pause to refresh himself or his passengers once the needs of his steed had been attended to.

Tom's uncle leaned over the car door. "You'll be on your way to Norwich, then?" he asked.

"Yes, my man, that's right," came the tart reply.

"Ah, I just wanted you to know that if when you gets there you find you've lost your wallet, you didn't leave it here at the Sorrel Horse," was the landlord's cutting retort.

Even in Tom's day the Sorrel Horse was an old-fashioned haven of calm in a troubled world. Tom, however, was able to look back to a time when it had been very much a centre of local affairs where farmers not only gathered to discuss the crops, the state of the weather and parish happenings but also came twice a year to pay their rent.

"All the tenants off the Shrubland estate used to come here to pay their rents and their tithe," he recalled. "They used to have the room out of the back there.

"We used to put on a feed for them, they used to have a feed in the back room before they had the money taken off them. They'd have come back the next day to have another feed, if they'd had the time," he added with a wink at one of his customers sitting in the corner.

Times had changed, though. Tom no longer catered for such gatherings, but was known to hob-nob with well-known personalities from other worlds who were taking the cure at the Shrubland Hall health clinic. "Notabilities from the other side of the road," he called them.

Small wonder that Lord de Saumarez came "from the other side of the road" to make a presentation to Tom when he retired. On behalf of the customers, of course.

By a strange coincidence, the Sorrel Horse still has a strong link with Tolly Cobbold since the landlady, Breda Smith, is one of the publican shareholders of today's brewery.

One Tolly Cobbold licensee was even able to claim that he had been born in the pub of which he became landlord. Cecil Cobbold was born at the Punch Bowl, Combs, then a Cobbold house, in 1904, a year or so after his parents, Frank and Ethel Cobbold, had moved there from the White Horse at Haughley. Cecil took over the licence on his father's death in 1941, and remained at the Punch Bowl for thirty-five years until his retirement in 1977.

When John Cobbold went to the Punch Bowl to present a

"So far she hasn't joined the chorus of witty jokes about inflation"

Local scenes featured in many of Giles's cartoons. This one shows one of the oldest public houses in Ipswich, the Woolpack at the junction of Tuddenham Road and Westerfield Road, which is why Giles presented it to his friends at Cliff Brewery.

retirement present to the other Mr Cobbold he found himself the recipient of a bottle of Cobbold & Son fine rum and a bottle of Cobbold & Company Lancer whisky. It is not recorded where Cecil Cobbold had hidden the two bottles, but it is known that Cobbold & Son's fine rum was last made towards the end of the 19th century and that Lancer whisky was last bottled in the 1930s. Mr John told Cecil and his wife Joan that he would keep both bottles unopened.

And what of Tolly Cobbold customers? They have a loyalty few other customers have, which is one reason why the brewery has survived the upheavals of the past twenty years.

When the Golden Lion in the High Street at Over, Cambridgeshire, closed down in 1974 ninety-four-year-old Ernest Few saw little use for the commemorative tankard given him by Tolly Cobbold area manager Bill Barlow. Ernie had lifted his first pint in the Golden Lion when he was a lad of sixteen and had been a customer ever since; not a bad record, seventy-eight years a customer at one pub, but Ernie wasn't looking forward to the future.

"You ask me what I'll do when the Golden Lion closes," he said. "Blowed if I'm going to walk after the stuff. Just have to buy a tin of cocoa, that's all."

Giles's dedication to Patrick Cobbold on the cartoon above.

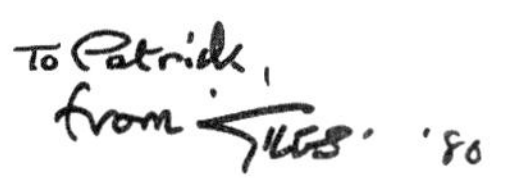

No story about Tolly Cobbold would be complete without a reference to Carl Giles, the *Daily Express* cartoonist, a close friend of the Cobbolds. Giles lived at Witnesham, not far from Ipswich, and there were many local people who recognised themselves in his cartoons from time to time; John Cobbold certainly appeared, though not necessarily in cartoons drawn for publication in the newspaper. He featured in at least one published cartoon, when he stood in an Ipswich by-election against Miss Manuela Sykes. He also appeared in a cartoon Giles drew for the programme of the Ipswich & Suffolk Licensed Trade Association banquet and ball in 1961; Giles was always willing to provide a drawing for his friends on such occasions. One suspects that John Cobbold, who was president of the Ipswich & Suffolk Licensed Trade Association, is also depicted on another Giles cartoon which today hangs in the offices in Cliff Cottage; one cannot be certain, as only a pair of feet are visible. Mr John would have been quite happy to have been so depicted; he was well known for telling jokes against himself.

The cover of the programme of Ipswich & Suffolk Licensed Trade Association's annual dinner and ball, drawn by Giles and showing John Cobbold "in the chair".

Mr John is not identified in this cartoon, but he was at the time the president of the Ipswich & Suffolk Licensed Trade Association. It seems fair to assume that it was this organisation's annual dinner for which Giles made this drawing.

The Tolly Cobbold management team, left to right, John Artiss, Chris Gregson, Sheila Moll, and Keith Blyth, outside Cliff Cottage.

Postscript: The Present and the Future

by the Hon. Peter Strutt, Chairman

I HAVE great pleasure in commending this Anniversary Book. A fascinating and intriguing element of this story is that it is a continuing story—the brewery is flourishing and is constantly planning and investing for the future.

Following the success of the Year Beers and the cask beers, Tollyshooter and Cobbold's IPA, new beers are being developed, tested and researched. During 1995, Cobbold's Conquest, a draught beer of yesteryear, was reintroduced and sales to date have been very encouraging.

At a time when some other regional brewers have moved out of brewing to concentrate on running pubs, the large investment in a new brewhouse at Tolly Cobbold is ample evidence of our commitment to brewing. It is a curiosity of timing that this new equipment should be commissioned almost 100 years after William Bradford built the "new" Cliff Brewery in 1896, incorporating the very latest in Victorian brewing technology.

The book has covered the role of **Brian Cowie** and **Bob Wales**, but I would like also to record my appreciation of all our loyal and dedicated employees and also our very professional Management Team.

Keith Blyth, the Commercial Manager, and his sales and telesales team are continuing to expand sales. A major export contract to Sweden has just been secured and plans are well under way to supply Tolly Cobbold beer to the United States.

John Artiss, the Operations Manager, is currently operating a daily fleet of sixteen 10-ton vehicles, not only to deliver Tolly Cobbold cask and bottled beer but also over 700 products for the licensed trade. In 1992, a distribution contract was secured to supply Carlsberg-Tetley products to their customers in Suffolk, North Essex and Cambridgeshire, and only last year this contract was extended to include Norfolk. The warehouse and transport crews are committed to providing a quality service, and in 1995 they were awarded the nationally recognised BS EN ISO 9002 quality award.

There have been no awards for **Sheila Moll**, the Accountant/Office Manager, and her staff, but nevertheless they have worked just as hard, and my sincere thanks to them.

Much has already been written on the brewery staff and our Head Brewer, **Chris Gregson**, but I am always impressed with their commitment to quality. Sir John recommended that we should look for a new slogan for our beer. Perhaps the old catchphrase "Tolly for quality" is one that we should reintroduce.

The last few years have seen difficult trading times for all breweries and for the licensed trade in general. One of the reasons for our success has been the loyalty of customers, and in repaying that loyalty the company has always tried to play its full part in the life of the community that we serve.

This book was commissioned not only to be a good read—and Bob Malster has done an excellent job on this—but also to record the history, the events and the people that have shaped Tolly Cobbold. As we look forward with confidence to our 300th anniversary, we can be pleased that the *250 Years of Brewing in Ipswich* has been appropriately celebrated.

Jamie Cann, MP, joins the men of Cliff Brewery to present a retirement gift to drayman Kenny Warren.

Index

Illustrations in bold type